Praise for
What Happens After Shattered?

"This book offers a great deal of solid information and helpful guidance based on the author's professional expertise. It is a unique and valuable resource for those in the Christian community as it fully integrates biblical teachings throughout the text."

—Peggy Vaughan, author of
To Have and To Hold and host of DearPeggy.com

"Dr. Deanna Sims has written a well thought out Christian counseling book on the topic of infidelity which will be of help to those in need of a faith-based self-help book on infidelity."

—Rona Subotnik, LMFT, co-author of *Surviving Infidelity,*
3rd Edition and author of *Why Did He Cheat on Me?*

"This book is a most welcome addition to Christian marriage therapy literature. Dr. Sims has constructed a lucid account of the path to healing from infidelity by seamlessly interweaving psychotherapeutic wisdom with scripture. Her compassion and sensitivity illuminate the pages of this book and provide a clear guide to the process of recovery."

—Dr. Pamela VanPelt-Tess, L.P.C., therapist in private practice

"Deanna offers both a clinical and a theological perspective on infidelity, to bring a reminder of God's love to the process of understanding and healing."

—Dr. C. Robert Hasley, Jr., Senior Pastor,
St. Andrew United Methodist Church, Plano, Texas.

"*What Happens After Shattered?* is a "standout" book on the issue of infidelity. Writing from the perspective of an experienced and talented psychotherapist, Dr. Deanna Sims defines and clarifies issues related to infidelity with depth and with reviews of some of the current studies in the field. She offers treatment planning for recovery and growth that is based on sound therapeutic principals as well as relevant scriptural support. She does all this while lovingly bearing witness to the healing power of God as she instructs both the hearts and minds of those who bear the pain of infidelity. I look forward to having this resource to recommend to patients in my own practice."

—Dr. Anne E. Andersen, psychiatrist, private practice

"Dr. Deanna Sims combines her clinical expertise with her Christian experience to provide wisdom, insight, and grace to those experiencing infidelity in marriage. Dr. Sims engages scripture and other prominent Christian theologians to shape a practical theology framework that can provide women a method for journeying through a difficult time. This book will be a valuable reference for me as a pastor when I meet with those who are needing practical therapeutic and theological direction."

—Reverend Kathryn Self Ransdell, United Methodist
Church Elder, Pastor, Vancouver, British Columbia

"Blending clinical expertise and a passion for forging growth from pain, Dr. Sims has produced a valuable resource for healing hearts and relationships shattered by infidelity. This book is filled with clinical examples and key spiritual truths that educate, encourage, and equip. For those navigating the arduous road of recovery and for professionals who are assisting them, *What Happens After Shattered?* is a must read!"

—Karla Hale Gerdes, Ph.D., Psychologist and
Licensed Marriage and Family Therapist, private practice

WHAT HAPPENS
AFTER SHATTERED?

WHAT HAPPENS AFTER SHATTERED?

Finding Hope and Healing After Infidelity

Dr. Deanna Sims

WESTBOW
PRESS®
A DIVISION OF THOMAS NELSON
& ZONDERVAN

scripture taken from the Holy Bible, New International Version®, NIV® Copyright© 1973, 1978, 1984, 2011 by Biblica, Inc.™ Used by permission of Zondervan. All rights reserved worldwide. WWW.ZONDERVAN.COM The "NIV" and "New International Version" are trademarks registered in the United States Patent and Trademark Offices by Biblica, Inc.™

Names and particular details of examples described in this book have been changed to protect the anonymity of the individuals.

WestBow Press books may be ordered through booksellers or by contacting:

WestBow Press
A Division of Thomas Nelson & Zondervan
1663 Liberty Drive
Bloomington, IN 47403
www.westbowpress.com
1 (866) 928-1240

ISBN: 978-1-4908-8817-0 (sc)
ISBN: 978-1-4908-8819-4 (hc)
ISBN: 978-1-4908-8818-7 (e)

Library of Congress Control Number: 2015914061

Print information available on the last page.

WestBow Press rev. date: 08/21/2015

To my parents, David and Marilyn Sims,
for always loving me unconditionally

Contents

Needing God the Most
Infidelity Statistics
Reasons for Continued Infidelity in our Culture
Infidelity: The Most Painful Experience
Reconciliation from Infidelity is Possible

Desire for Vindication and Validation
Anger as Part of the Healing and Grieving Process
Mountaintop Phenomenon
Anger is Morally Neutral
Anger and Negativity
Anger and Bitterness
Anger and Forgiveness
Anger: Righteous or Self-Righteous?

Validation of Anger
Tug of War Process of Forgiveness
Anger as Part of the Process of Forgiveness
Purging Type of Disclosure that Impacts Forgiveness
"Trickle Truth" Phenomenon
Truth is Necessary for Healing
The Right of Betrayed Spouses to Ask Questions

Supplementation to the Marriage
Reconnection with Former Lovers
Areas for Further Research
        Different Race of the Affair Partner

Definition of Vulnerability Factors
Indentifying Vulnerability Factors as an Affair-Prevention
Strategy
Communicating about Vulnerability Factors
Developing Strategies to Combat Vulnerability Factors
Adapting to Permanent Vulnerability Factors
Writing Plans to Battle Vulnerability Factors
Statistics for Straying Spouses on Bercht's Vulnerability Scale
Examples of Vulnerability Factors in One Couple
        Job Loss
        Temporary Financial Strain Due to Unemployment
        Death of a Grandparent
        Birth of Twin Babies
        Sexual Dysfunction
        History of a Parent's Affair
        Low Self-Esteem and Need for Admiration from Others
        Penchant for Pornography and Strip Club Attendance
        Child's Medical Problem
        Hesitancy to Discuss the Affairs
Classification of Vulnerability Factors: Short-Term, Long-Term,
Chronic, and Permanent
Exploring Vulnerability Factors in Detail: One Couple's Analysis
and Plan

Prayer
        First Documented Prayer in the Bible: Eve
        Second Documented Prayer in the Bible: Cain
        Prayer as a Step Toward Healing After Infidelity
        Prayers of Petition

Encourage Mentorship Programs
between Senior and Junior Employees for
Accountability
Host Affair-Prevention Seminars in the
Workplace
Establish a No-Penalty-for-Honesty Policy
Arrange Projects in Threes

Highlights the Conflicts Within an Individual and in the
Marriage
Catalyst for Getting Couples into Therapy
Forces Communication Which Can Foster Greater
Intimacy
Suffering Can Be Transformed to Hope
Opportunity to Display Forgiveness and Mercy
Ability to Become More Christlike Through Pain and
Suffering
Opportunity to Show Good Behavior in Times of
Adversity

AUTHOR'S NOTE

This book is written to benefit several different audiences. First, it is written to provide hope and encouragement to betrayed spouses who have just learned that their mate has been unfaithful. Whether you choose to stay married and reconcile your relationship or divorce and begin a life on your own, this book is for you. Second, it is to appeal to couples who wish to repair and reconcile their marriages after the discovery of infidelity. Third, this is a book for all couples wishing to learn more about the dynamics of infidelity in hopes of preserving and safeguarding their relationships from the shattering pain of affairs. The book educates readers, arming them with the facts about infidelity and defenses against it. Fourth, it is a book for clergy and mental health professionals who desire to help people in crisis and who want to be a part of the healing journey for people who have experienced infidelity.

Statistics show that more men are unfaithful to their wives than women are to their husbands. I have tried to use case examples from both genders, but have probably used more language depicting the betrayed spouse as female to correspond to current statistics. In Chapter 5, I used the pronoun "he" exclusively because Narcissism is gender specific, with 75 percent of diagnosed individuals being male.

In this book, infidelity is defined as:

"a breach of trust in a committed relationship, whether emotional, sexual, or both."

Although many of the examples in the book will be addressing sexual infidelity, the pain and suffering of emotional infidelity is just as devastating. Many people report that it is not so much the sexual indiscretions that are so painful to tolerate, but the dishonesty and deceit that generate the most feelings of anguish after discovery.

This book is interspersed with scripture that I greatly treasure. The most gratifying part of writing this manuscript for me was researching biblical texts. I hope that reading the scriptural passages are as inspiring for you as they were for me. I do not think people can effectively mature through a time of suffering without God's divine revelation, so when writing this book, it felt incomplete to leave out what seemed so obvious and imperative: the importance of scripture in providing hope, healing, and growth. If you are not a person of faith or are mad at God for permitting infidelity to occur, you are not alone. When reading this book, I invite you to evaluate all of your options for support, and consider a relationship with God as a source of comfort. So often we find ourselves at odds with God when suffering occurs and it challenges our own sense of entitlement for a happy life for following the rules.

There is not necessarily a recommended way to read the book. Some may benefit from reading it cover to cover, whereas others may browse the table of contents and select a chapter that pertains to a specific need during a time of desperation. My recommendation is to follow your heart.

I have purposely chosen the style of book and chapter titles for specific reasons. Additionally, case examples will afford you with true-to-life circumstances to aid in your understanding of infidelity. My desire was to design a triad of sorts, a trifecta of healing in this book. Thus, I address infidelity from a psychological stance, the spiritual perspective, along with educational components. Discussion questions appear at the end of each chapter for individual examination or group dialogue.

The first chapter provides statistics about infidelity and describes the nature of pain associated with infidelity. Chapter 2 on anger is a must-read, because that seems to be the universal feeling experienced by many when dealing with infidelity. Forgiveness also seemed to be a necessary part for the book, for one cannot move forward out of the anger without the process of forgiveness described in Chapter 3.

Chapter 4 is a psycho-educational chapter on the types of affairs. Education is crucial to understanding affair behavior and I believe that knowledge is power. Equipping yourself with information aids you in moving forward in your healing process. Something different about this book that I haven't seen in many infidelity books is the inclusion of a special historical section about the infamous, sexual libertine character of Don Juan. I found it fascinating to throw in some history as I learned how his notorious behavior has persisted over generations. Nearly one hundred works of art and literature have been created to portray his licentious character.

Chapter 5 gives you information about narcissism because this trait, according to research, correlates with susceptibility to infidelity. Education about symptoms of narcissism can equip you with information to aid you in understanding whether the straying spouse carries this disorder.

Chapter 6 focuses on the specific process of discovery of infidelity and gives case examples. Chapter 7 discusses the importance of refusing to suffer in silence and the fundamental importance of transparency and total and complete honesty. Chapter 7 also discusses disclosure of the affair and to whom to reveal the infidelity: God, counselors, family, friends, and children. There are case examples of different couples and whether or not they chose to disclose the affair to their children, often an agonizing decision.

Chapter 8 is a chapter specifically about the affair partner and how the affair partner is often selected. Chapter 9 addresses the definition and variable length of vulnerability factors and strategies to address them after an affair is discovered. An interview with author Brian Bercht and his self-developed vulnerability scale is also mentioned in this chapter. A Vulnerability Factor Worksheet is designed for you to address your own vulnerability factors and is located in the back of the book in Appendix B.

Chapter 10 is a comprehensive chapter about caring for the betrayed spouse following infidelity. Oftentimes, when people are suffering, they forget to take care of themselves, so this chapter is very important. Specific skills that will be addressed include prayer, therapy, medication, exercise, journaling, support groups, bibliotherapy, and nurturing activities. I have created a list of one hundred nurturing activities that I would be delighted for you to try. They are listed in Appendix A at the end of the book.

Chapter 11 is a chapter about recovery and affair-prevention. This chapter suggests recovery strategies; specifically, ways to safeguard your marriage to prevent the likelihood of future affairs. There is a special section on preventing affairs in the workplace in this chapter, too.

Chapter 12, the final chapter, is about the unexpected "benefits" of affairs. This chapter addresses how the pain of affairs can ultimately be transformed for the betterment of relationships. God can take something so impure, such as infidelity, work His miracle of transcendence, and, with time, the pain of a partner's affair can be transformed into hope.

My desire is that you enjoy reading this book as much as I enjoyed writing it.

Blessings and Peace,

Dr. Deanna Sims

Acknowledgments

Thank you God for providing opportunities in my life from which I can learn, build character, become closer to You, and help others heal. Thank you to my wonderful parents, Dr. David and Marilyn Sims, who have always loved me unconditionally.

Thank you to all who served on my lay editing team. Thank you to Dr. Karla Hale Gerdes, my lead editor. Thank you, Karla, for all your time and helpful comments, your biblical expertise, and your friendship. Thank you for helping me choose the title of the book. Thank you to the rest of the editing team for proofing my manuscript during its many revisions: David and Marilyn Sims, Merv and Helen Stauffer, Bob and Jan Gillespie, Lida Lindley, Doug and Claudia Weiler, Kelli Karlow, Christa Richardson, Dr. Michelle Richards, Connie Cole, Londa Wilder, Catherine Ogie, and Dayne Albert.

Thank you to the ladies of Kings Ridge Bible Study: Lida Lindley, Claudia Weiler, Kelli Karlow, Apryl Iley, Pam Fernando, Amy Kowalchyk, Kristy Kinzley, and Sandy Weissinger. I cherish your prayers and your endless support and friendship.

Thank you to Kathy Sutherland for introducing me to authors like Adam Hamilton and Leslie Weatherhead.

Thank you to all the authors who have encouraged and supported my passion and mission to help those impacted by infidelity: Peggy Vaughan, Rona Subotnik, Dr. Greg Swenson, and Dr. Sam Vaknin. Thank you to Brian Bercht for granting me an interview so I could learn more about his self-developed vulnerability scale.

Thank you to my Aunt Mary Womack for reaching out to me. Thank you to my cousin and publicist, Carol Perry, for all of your marketing and advertising expertise.

Thank you to my friends for your wisdom, support, and guidance: Debbie Cooney, Dr. Pam VanPelt-Tess, Lida Lindley, Claudia Weiler, Kelli Karlow, Lin Taylor, Bob and Jan Gillespie, and Merv and Helen Stauffer.

Chapter 1

INFIDELITY

Her world as she knew it had been shattered. Her heart was broken into a million tiny pieces. The rug had been pulled out from underneath her and she never saw it coming. What happened? The shock, confusion, the nausea and sleepless nights, and the torment and anger riddled her with constant obsessive thinking. The power of love, or what she thought was love, had been compromised. The surreptitiously concealed affairs were quite horrifying and incompatible with her cherished internal value system of "'til death do we part." She had truly believed the words he told her at the altar and now she had begun to question the whole marriage, her trust in relationships with others, and what was right side up and upside down. This was a time when she yearned more for God and was desperate for answers.

Although infidelity changes life dramatically, God is the one true thing who remains constant and faithful. He is the divine healer and may eventually reveal how the journey of recovering from an affair can become one of your greatest spiritual victories. This triumph often provides the building blocks for more passion, perseverance, and hope in a new life to come. You can emerge from the shock and shattering pain of infidelity through recovery and healing, which can unexpectedly lead to a powerful renewal of life.

Infidelity

Infidelity is on the rise. Although the majority of our culture supports monogamy, it paradoxically continues to condone infidelity. Exact numbers are difficult to deduce because of underreporting, the secretiveness of affairs, and the shame associated with infidelity. Tom Smith (2003) wrote a report on the findings from *The General Social Survey* at the National Opinion Research Center located at the University of Chicago which concluded that 15 to 18 percent of individuals have an extramarital relationship during the course of their marriage. On the other hand, Peggy Vaughan (2003), author of *The Monogamy Myth: A Personal Handbook for Recovery from Affairs*, reported that conservative estimates suggest that 60 percent of men and 40 percent of women have extramarital affairs. Regardless of the discrepancy in statistics, infidelity is a copious problem in a society that incongruently claims to value monogamy. It is my guess that several phenomena contribute to the prevalence of extramarital affairs despite the stated preferred value of monogamy:

- Breakdown of the institution of marriage
- Multiple marital vulnerabilities (increased stressors in today's society)
- Reduced stigma of divorce
- Increase in cultural entitlement
- Media sensationalism of affairs
- Increase of workplace affairs
- More women in the workplace

Infidelity is one of the most painful and traumatic experiences one can encounter. Sexual betrayal exposes our most instinctual need for love, trust, and secure belonging. When people experience the palpable and visceral pain of infidelity, their sense of self-worth, feeling loved, and the very essence of belonging have been shattered. One individual's report in Dr. Janis Abrahms Spring's (1996) book *After the Affair* described her partner's infidelity as more painful than when she was raped as a child. Rona Subotnik, L.M.F.T. and Dr. Gloria Harris, (2005) authors of *Surviving Infidelity: Making Decisions, Recovering from the Pain*, metaphorically describe the intense emotions of infidelity like an erupting volcano.

Infidelity breaks trust, shatters hearts, and wreaks havoc on marriages. Infidelity leaves an unforgettable imprint on the hearts and in the minds of both betrayed spouses and straying spouses. Infidelity is a life changing event.

While dealing with one of the most emotionally and psychologically devastating experiences, restoring a broken marriage after an affair takes time, effort, and hard work. Although infidelity is the leading cause of divorce according to Dr. David M. Buss (2000), author of *The Dangerous Passion: Why Jealousy Is as Necessary as Love and Sex*, the good news holds that most marriages sustain extramarital affairs. Repair of a shattered heart and a broken marriage is possible. Repair requires forgiveness, vulnerability, and practicing trust on the betrayed spouse's part and complete honesty and disclosure, and demonstrating trust on the straying spouse's part. My earnest desire is for all marriages to be preserved; however, I know in reality that is not always possible. Faithfulness and honesty are necessities and prerequisites for a healthy, sustainable marriage. This is what God intended when He created marriage. God says, "Drink waters out of thine own cistern, and running waters out of thine own well" (Proverbs 5:15 KJV).

Discussion Questions

1. On a scale of one (mild) to ten (severe), rate how painful your infidelity experience has been.
2. How do you feel when the media exposes affairs of politicians or celebrities?
3. Do you think the rise in divorce rates over the past few decades has contributed to the increase in infidelity?
4. Do you believe that reconciliation is possible after an affair?

CHAPTER 2

ANGER

Feelings of anger and the desire for validation and vindication following infidelity are perfectly normal and human. Some women suffer in silence and do not allow themselves to show anger because of family of origin prescriptions (e.g., what happens in the family stays in the family), cultural messages that denounce the expression of women's anger, or fears of displeasing their spouses or others. When you are hurt deeply or violated and traumatized after an extramarital affair, it is universal to desire a conviction after being unjustly treated. The hurt and pain following the discovery of an affair is often expressed via anger. It is quite common and normal to feel angry, and rightfully so, after your marital commitment is violated in the most fundamental way.

Allow yourself permission to feel angry as part of your healing process. To begin mending your broken heart, validate your anger with creative language, self-empathy, and the art of compassion by acknowledging your pronounced state of anger. Anger is often an outward expression of underlying hurt and fear. Anger is a normal phase of grieving and often pushes one out of sadness and depression. It can sometimes be the impetus to get one moving to provide more self-care, to set boundaries, or to be assertive for the first time.

God made us and gave us feelings, much like His own. "Then God said, 'Let us make man in our image, in our likeness . . .'" (Genesis 1:26 NIV). Moreover, scripture tells us that at times God Himself felt angry. Therefore, if it is acceptable for Him to feel anger, it must be acceptable for us to feel anger.

- "I have seen these people," the LORD said to Moses, "and they are a stiffnecked people. Now leave me alone so that my anger may burn against them and that I may destroy them. Then I will make you into a great nation." Exodus 32:9-10 (NIV)

- The LORDS's anger was aroused that day and he swore this oath: Because they have not followed me wholeheartedly, not one of the men twenty years old or more who came up out of Egypt will see the land I promised on oath to Abraham, Isaac and Jacob . . . Numbers 32:10-11 (NIV)
- The LORDS's anger burned against Israel and he made them wander in the desert forty years, until the whole generation of those who had done evil in his sight was gone. Numbers 32:13 (NIV)
- In furious anger and in great wrath the LORD uprooted them from their land and thrust them into another land, as it is now. Deuteronomy 29:28 (NIV)
- Go and inquire of the LORD for me and for the people and for all of Judah about what is written in this book that has been found: Great is the LORD's anger that burns against us because our fathers have not obeyed the words of this book; they have not acted in accordance with all that is written there concerning us. II Kings 22:13 (NIV)

Mountaintop Phenomenon

Many betrayed spouses experience a *mountaintop phenomenon.* This is a metaphoric term used to describe the desire to "shout from a mountaintop" one's experience for all to hear or know. The purpose of the exclamation is to claim validation or vindication. This need for vindication connected to anger is righteous anger after being wronged by infidelity. Anger is a very therapeutic emotion, an emotion that is morally neutral. Repeat: anger is *morally* neutral. In addition, anger is valid and justified like any other emotion. All emotions are morally neutral. Where anger receives its negative reputation can be in its behavioral expression, which is not always morally neutral. Harming yourself or others is not morally neutral because this crosses the moral threshold of respect for personal and interpersonal boundaries.

Although the emotion of anger is morally neutral, it is not emotionally neutral. Anger falls under the negative umbrella of emotions. When spouses have been wronged or are grieving a loss, anger is a necessary, temporary emotional state for them to experience. Notice I say the word *temporary.* Betrayed spouses who get stuck in anger will experience an inability to forgive and a buildup of bitterness. Whether the marriage stays intact or terminates, it is important that you arrive at a place of forgiveness for your own health and wellness. Bitterness and lack of forgiveness can lead to other obstacles in your life, such as pessimistic attitudes toward relationships, negative self-talk or self-image, and social isolation. Cultivate a desire and make a goal to change bitterness to *betterness*. Although it is necessary to feel and acknowledge your anger, notice in scripture the instructions God gives regarding how long to experience anger and what to do with anger.

- The LORD is slow to anger, abounding in love and forgiving sin and rebellion. Numbers 14:18 (NIV)
- For his anger lasts only a moment, but his favor lasts a lifetime . . . Psalm 30:5 (NIV)
- Yet he was merciful; he forgave their iniquities and did not destroy them. Time after time he restrained his anger and did not stir up his full wrath. Psalm 78:38 (NIV)
- A fool gives full vent to his anger, but a wise man keeps himself under control. Proverbs 29:11 (NIV)
- Be ye angry, and sin not: let not the sun go down upon your wrath . . . Ephesians 4:26 (KJV)
- My dear brothers, take note of this: Everyone should be quick to listen, slow to speak, and slow to become angry, for man's anger does not bring about the righteous life that God desires. James 1:19-20 (NIV)

Anger: Righteous or Self-Righteous?

In her book *Companions in Christ: The Way of Forgiveness*, Marjorie Thompson (2002) noted the "multifaceted" nature of anger with its advantages and disadvantages. Righteous anger is anger which we feel when we or others have been wronged by someone else. Richard Strauss (1991), author of *Growing More Like Jesus: A Practical Guide to Developing a Christlike Character*, noted Jesus felt righteous indignation when the greed of the Sadducees exploited the needy, contributed to the misuse of the holy temple, and distorted the truth. In the Bible, the Pharisees and Sadducees were two groups known for intellectually keeping the law. But at a heart level, they often fell short because of their preoccupation with legalities. They often challenged one another about who knew best. Jesus was angry about their exploitation of others, and the obstacles they created for would-be worshippers at the temple.

> In the temple courts he found men selling cattle, sheep and doves, and others sitting at tables exchanging money. So he made a whip out of cords, and drove all from the temple area, both sheep and cattle; he scattered the coins of the money changers and overturned their tables. To those who sold doves he said, "Get these out of here! How dare you turn my Father's house into a market!" John 2:14-16 (NIV)

How can we tell if our anger is righteous or self-righteous? "Righteous" refers to God's true standards for right and wrong. Thompson (2002) suggested three strategies to help individuals discern the difference between righteous and self-righteous anger. First, she suggested exploring your level of personal integrity. Ask yourself if you practice what you preach. Do you have the same expectations of yourself as you do for others? Do you follow the same rules you lay out for other people? Do you behave in ways you want others to treat you? If the answers to these questions are yes, then you are on the right track. If the answers are no, then you have some reevaluating to do.

The second suggestion by Thompson (2002) regarding discernment between righteous and self-righteous anger is to demonstrate a sincere spirit of humility. Being able to look within oneself and admit weaknesses and faults is a sign of maturity and wisdom. Maturity and wisdom can foster a spirit of humility which protects against bravado, self-righteous anger, and blind spots regarding one's own character.

Third, Thompson (2002) challenged individuals to assess whether or not their anger interfered with their fundamental belief in God. The greatest Commandment reads "Love the Lord your God with all your heart and with all your soul and with all your mind. This is the first and greatest commandment" (Matthew 22:37-38 NIV). Essentially, if your anger is interfering with your ability to love, pray, or worship the Lord, then it is not righteous anger.

Case Example

Allen, a thirty-two-year-old engineer, learned his wife of seven years had had an affair early in their marriage. He realized the importance of not letting his anger and condemnation of his wife get the best of him. Although his wife described him as feeling angry from time to time, the first scripture he quoted her following discovery was, " . . . if any one of you is without sin, let him be the first to throw a stone at her" (John 8:7 NIV). Allen knew fundamentally that to stay stuck in his anger and to condemn his wife would be counterproductive to the reconciliation of his marriage.

Discussion Questions

1. How did you express your anger after you learned about your spouse's affair?
2. Did you experience anger emotionally, physically, or both?
3. Were you able to identify any underlying feelings beneath the anger (i.e., hurt, fear)?
4. How are anger and forgiveness connected?

CHAPTER 3

FORGIVENESS

To address anger one must first validate it and then let go of it through the journey of forgiveness. People cannot do this alone and therefore must call upon the help of the Lord during this process. Forgiveness does not come instinctually to humans. For many, it is akin to a tug-of-war process. Anger is often the raw ingredient that leads to the process of transformation. The decision whether to forgive is precipitated by an injustice marked by intense feelings of hurt and anger. Therefore, injustices are often opportunities for betrayed spouses to examine their own reactions. The process of forgiveness can mend a heart shattered by infidelity.

Case Example

One couple, John, a fifty-three-year-old stockbroker, married to Sharon, a forty-seven-year-old surgical nurse, had been together for twelve years. After years of repetitive lying to his spouse, John finally admitted an affair after he was confronted with indisputable evidence. When he finally confessed his betrayal after days of lying, his admission came out as a purging type of disclosure. He revealed multiple sexual transgressions. This required Sharon to acknowledge there were more problems to forgive than she had originally expected. She had some important decisions to make. After discovery and disclosure, John decided to attend an accountability group at church. He revealed his transgressions to others, demonstrating honesty, and made a commitment to join Sex and Love Addicts Anonymous (SLAA). Sharon forgave John, they attended couples therapy, and slowly began to rebuild trust and strengthen the integrity in the relationship. Two years later, their relationship is fragile, but headed in the right direction. Forgiveness was needed, along with John's desire to change, for their relationship to be reconciled, for forgiveness alone is necessary, but not sufficient, for reconciliation.

John released information only after Sharon's confrontation, when she showed him receipts from a hotel he had booked with a lover. It is common for straying spouses to discharge or unload information after carrying around secrets for months, sometimes years. Perhaps the guilt and shame has become quite burdensome to them and they need an emotional release. It is uncommon for them to be completely honest upon the first disclosure, for they tend to withhold details and only reveal the absolute minimum to protect themselves. The truth seems to be revealed over time, a phenomenon well-known as the "trickle truth." Many straying spouses claim they are protecting the betrayed spouse and sparing them from the hurtful details, yet they are really only protecting themselves from their own guilt and shame or desire to evade exposure.

Most experts suggest that total honesty and transparency are the best methods for preserving the integrity of a relationship. It is not fair for the straying spouse to withhold information and "assume" what the betrayed spouse can tolerate. Furthermore, if details are left out and then later exposed, a feeling of secrecy and mistrust develops all over again, undermining what repair work has been done on the relationship.

After discovery of an affair, the truth must come out for complete healing to take place for both parties if reconciliation is desired. The betrayed spouse has a right to ask questions and understand details that she desires to know, and the straying spouse needs to be accountable and completely honest in order for growth, development, and changes in behavior to take place. Because the truth may emerge in spurts, the betrayed spouse may experience hurt and betrayal multiple times. This means that she may also have to choose forgiveness multiple times, which can be an emotional and spiritual challenge for many. Because the truth may come out in fragments, forgiveness may also be revealed in spurts.

Although the truth is necessary for healing and reconciliation, it is important for the betrayed spouse to consider what specific questions to ask. Some desire to know specific sexual details of the affair, for to not know renders them feeling helpless and powerless. Contrarily, some desire not to know specific sexual details, for fear they will be painfully etched in memory for a lifetime. Individuals must decide for themselves what information will be helpful for personal healing.

Much like faithfulness is a necessary requisite for the straying spouse to redevelop, forgiveness must be a condition that the betrayed spouse cultivates. The reconciliation process requires each partner to be working on different relationship issues to contribute to the effective rebuilding of the marriage. In other words, the straying spouse works on faithfulness and honesty, while the betrayed spouse works on being vulnerable and forgiving.

Forgiveness is a necessary condition for a betrayed spouse to cultivate, whether reconciling the marriage or terminating and filing for divorce. Some betrayed spouses do not get all their affair questions answered and therefore do not receive closure or complete and total honesty from the straying spouse. If you are separating from your straying spouse, please know that forgiveness is necessary for your own personal growth, but the truth, although desirable, is not necessary for your personal healing. If reconciling, then both forgiveness from the betrayed and truthfulness from the straying spouse are necessary for marital restoration and reconciliation.

Myths of Forgiveness

Myth 1: Forgiveness means forgetting.

Myth 2: Forgiveness means continuing an unhealthy relationship.

Myth 3: Forgiveness symbolizes personal weakness.

Myth 4: Forgiveness condones the negative behavior.

Myth 5: Only certain sins are unforgiveable.

Many individuals experience conflict about forgiveness. Forgiveness does not mean forgetting, a common myth. Likewise, forgiveness does not always mean continuation of the relationship, although my preference, stated previously in Chapter 1, is for a marriage to stay intact, if at all possible, which is God's design. This plan requires both partners to be willing to work on having a healthy, committed, monogamous relationship. Moreover, forgiveness does not symbolize weakness or surrendering of values. In other words, it does not condone the behaviors of the straying spouse. Rather, forgiveness relinquishes the anger and need for retribution from the betrayed spouse. Furthermore, without exception, there is no unforgiveable sin, despite the inordinate amount of suffering and heartache it may have caused. This blanket of forgiveness covers the sin of adultery, the seventh Commandment, specifically provided by God in His Ten Commandments—the comprehensive set of rules to guide our lives.

Many betrayed spouses feel myriad emotions: hurt, devastation, betrayal, confusion, shock, grief, and anger. These are normal feelings following the discovery of an affair, but to move beyond the pain, forgiveness is the key ingredient for the recipe of healing to begin. The following scriptures are for you to meditate on to help you reach a place of forgiveness:

- And forgive us our debts, as we forgive our debtors. Matthew 6:12 (KJV)
- Bear with each other and forgive whatever grievances you may have against one another. Forgive as the Lord forgave you. Colossians 3:13 (NIV)
- Then Peter came to Jesus and asked, "Lord how many times shall I forgive my brother when he sins against me? Up to seven times?" Jesus answered, "I tell you, not seven times, but seventy-seven times." Matthew 18:21-22 (NIV)
- . . . Receive the Holy Spirit. If you forgive anyone his sins, they are forgiven; if you do not forgive them, they are not forgiven. John 20:22-23 (NIV)
- The punishment inflicted on him by the majority is sufficient for him. Now instead, you ought to forgive and comfort him, so that he will not be overwhelmed by excessive sorrow. II Corinthians 2:6-7(NIV)
- He told them, "This is what is written: The Christ will suffer and rise from the dead on the third day, and repentance and forgiveness of sins will be preached in his name to all nations . . . Luke 24:46-47(NIV)

Feelings of anger can come in spurts and challenge your understanding of forgiveness. Most people are familiar with the concept of forgiveness, yet the pain of infidelity hurts so deeply and often feels incompatible and incongruent with forgiveness. One betrayed spouse noted it took her eighteen months before she could say the words "I love you" again to her husband. The fear of being hurt again often prohibits forgiveness and learning to be vulnerable with your spouse can often take months or years. For some, the act of forgiveness feels like a competition: anger and protection on one team and mercy and forgiveness on the other. Anger can sometimes stand in the way of the completion of the forgiveness process. In other words, it can act like a barrier, perhaps a protective defense mechanism against hurt, holding some back from the transforming, healing benefits of forgiveness.

I challenge the reader to consider this: *"Can one forgive someone and still be angry? Why or why not?"* More specifically, *"Does one need to have worked through anger completely before total forgiveness can take place?"* Write your thoughts here:

_____

_____

_____

_____

_____

_____

_____

Forgiveness rarely comes easily and it seems to be a *process* rather than an event, even though some desire it to be a finished result from the beginning. What this suggests to me is a reminder that as children of God we are weak, fallible, and utterly dependent on Him. "He remembered that they were but flesh, a passing breeze that does not return" (Psalm 78:39 NIV). Forgiveness is available only through the Holy Spirit, who equips us with the gift of offering forgiveness. We are unable to do it on our own merit or by our own accord.

- My salvation and honor depend on God; he is my mighty rock, my refuge. Psalm 62:7 (NIV)
- I can do all things through Christ which strengtheneth me. Philippians 4:13 (KJV)

- I am the vine; you are the branches. If a man remains in me and I in him, he will bear much fruit; apart from me you can do nothing. John 15:5 (NIV)

Discussion Questions

1. Why do you think some people are more willing to forgive than others?
2. Does forgiveness suggest a personality characteristic of a "pleaser?"
3. Does forgiveness suggest a particular religious value?
4. Do you believe that infidelity is forgivable?
5. Does lack of forgiveness indicate holding a grudge?
6. Does forgiveness symbolize a closer connection with God?
7. What are the obstacles for you in forgiving your straying spouse?
8. Is forgiveness easier if your spouse voluntarily confessed to the affair versus you finding out on your own?

CHAPTER 4

TYPES OF INFIDELITY

Affairs present themselves in many different ways. An affair can be an emotional breach of trust in a committed relationship or a sexual infringement upon vows in a committed relationship, or involve both. Three things that all affairs share in common are secrecy, lies, and violation of trust. Upon interviewing women in an infidelity support group, many said that their husbands having sex with another woman was secondary, and it was the lying and the breach of emotional trust that their husbands violated that was so deeply hurtful. Dr. Frank Pittman (1989), author of *Private Lies: Infidelity and the Betrayal of Intimacy*, wrote, "It isn't whom you lie with. It's whom you lie to" (p. 53).

In this chapter, I will describe four common types of infidelity and discuss sexual addiction symptoms. Exit affairs and retaliatory affairs will be discussed later in Chapter 8. As a betrayed spouse it is important to educate yourself about the types of extramarital affairs and sexual addiction symptoms in case you are struggling with any self-blame. Being educated about types of infidelity and addiction symptoms can help categorize affair behavior to remind you that the person who had the affair is responsible for the affair. In other words the betrayed spouse is *never* responsible for the affair. Only the people who engaged in the affair are responsible for the affair. Since a betrayed spouse does not *make* a straying spouse commit adultery, she cannot *make* a spouse stop the affair, either. Moreover, lack of responsibility for the affair also renders betrayed spouses powerless to cease or prohibit affair behaviors of their spouses. This often contributes to feelings of helplessness for the betrayed if the straying spouse wishes to continue sexual indiscretions. Although feelings of helplessness are normal in a traumatic situation, such as infidelity, note that you do have choices regarding how you react and respond, even if you don't have control over your straying spouse's behaviors.

Additionally, Pittman (1989) noted that it is an individual choice regarding how to deal with marital dissatisfaction. In other words, each person in the marriage is responsible for how he or she chooses to cope with marital difficulties. The straying spouse could choose therapy, prayer, attending a marital workshop, speaking to a minister, talking to friends, or even divorce if the relationship is so dissatisfying. Ultimately, affairs are individual choices. Pittman (1989) suggested that affairs may be a way for the straying spouse to highlight trouble spot(s) in the marriage. This theory can be useful for therapists to explore when identifying problem areas in the relationship post-discovery during the healing phase of reconciliation.

It is acceptable to look within yourself and explore marital dynamics, personality issues, or vulnerability factors (which I will discuss in Chapter 9), and how those may have contributed to marital problems. Keep in mind that affairs are unhealthy behaviors; specifically, maladaptive responses to stress, marital problems, or unresolved family of origin wounds. **All marriages have problems, but not all marriages have affairs**. Therefore, we can draw a conclusion that people have choices, and individuals who have marital problems are capable of coping in alternative ways besides choosing infidelity.

Note to Therapists

It is important for therapists to understand this concept that betrayed spouses have no causal role in the affair. The worst question a therapist could ask the betrayed spouse is "What was your role in the affair?" The betrayed spouse had no role in the affair, because the affair took place between the straying spouse and the affair partner. Carder (1992) described a case example in which a therapist recommended a betrayed spouse "own" her role in the affair. This is not therapeutic language. The betrayed spouse may "own" her role of problems and responsibilities in the marriage, but therapists should never suggest that the betrayed spouse take ownership for the affair itself, for that is contradictory and confusing for patients. (Other than this one criticism, I enjoyed Carder's book.) A more therapeutic question would be "What were some of the vulnerability factors in the relationship during or preceding the affair?" Pittman (1989) noted that one cannot "make" a spouse commit infidelity, and since affairs are usually secret, the physical absence of the betrayed is required.

Peggy Vaughan (2010), author of *Helping Therapists (and their clients) in Dealing with Affairs,* developed a free online book for therapists who work with couples dealing with infidelity. During a lifetime of dedication to and research on affair recovery, Vaughan surveyed 1, 083 individuals whose spouses had had affairs and found several useful findings for therapists. Vaughan (2010) reported that 47 percent of the respondents saw three or more therapists following their spouse's affair and 57 percent reported feeling frustrated with their providers. She further learned that 23 percent of therapists did not encourage honest communication about the affair and 59 percent of therapists focused on general marital issues in lieu of the affair. Vaughan (2010) summarized multiple anecdotes of respondents in her book and formulated eleven major points for therapists to consider when treating couples dealing with infidelity. Her findings from the survey indicate some powerful fundamentals for therapists to infuse into the therapeutic process when working with those struggling with infidelity.

- Deal directly with the affair, not just ordinary marital counseling
- Deal with the emotional impact of the affair
- Don't "blame" the affair on the hurt spouse
- Be supportive of those couples who want to try to save the marriage
- Don't keep secrets or too quickly believe the lies of the one who had the affair
- See both parties together
- Be aware of the impact of your gender/beliefs/experiences on therapy
- Don't expect the hurt party to forget the affair or "set it aside and go on"
- Help clients connect with others who have "been there"
- Be well-informed about affairs and provide good information
- Encourage honest communication and answering all questions

(Vaughan, 2010, p. 46)

Therapists are the encouragers of hope when all else has failed in the relationship. They are the choreographers of a post-affair treatment plan to help couples identify individual and marital vulnerabilities that threaten the sacredness of marriage. Therapists have an important role to help couples rebuild relationships and therefore are the keepers of marital preservation. They are also the supporters and healers of individuals who, for whatever reason, choose divorce rather than reconciliation.

Classifying Infidelity

Subotnik and Harris (2005) suggested another reason for understanding what type of affair your partner has had is to determine the seriousness of the emotional investment of the straying spouse in the affair partner. This helps you determine where the straying spouse's loyalty lies, which ultimately aids you in determining if the marriage is salvageable. Following are four types of affairs they have described: the fling, the serial affair, the romantic affair, and the long-term affair.

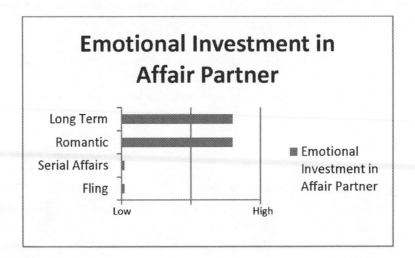

The Fling

The first type of affair they describe is the fling, often known as the "one night stand." Though it can be longer in duration, it is a relatively short term affair. This type of affair is portrayed by lack of emotional commitment to the sexual partner (Subotnik & Harris, 2005). The straying spouse typically has no desire to leave the marriage, and has no desire to commit or invest with the sexual partner. The fling is often impulsive, reckless, or hedonistic, feeding immediate needs without regard to future consequences. Although very painful upon discovery, the fling is considered to be the least serious of the four types of affairs (Subotnik & Harris, 2005). Because the emotional commitment of a fling is relatively low, the likelihood of the marriage being salvageable is greater. That said, it is very important to see the fling as a warning sign and assess accurately for remorse and changed behavior so the fling does not exacerbate into serial affairs.

Serial Affairs

Serial affairs are repetitive affairs over the course of a marriage with different sexual partners. People who have affairs are more likely to repeat affair behaviors, since they have chosen it as a coping skill when feeling unhappy or dissatisfied. Men are more likely to have multiple affairs, compared to women. Dr. Lana Staheli (1995), author of *"Affair-Proof" Your Marriage: Understanding, Preventing and Surviving an Affair*, reported that two thirds of men who had affairs had multiple affairs, 25 percent of men who had affairs had four or more affairs, and 15 percent of women who had affairs typically had on average between one and three.

Individuals cheat for a variety of reasons, so it is important to understand all the vulnerability factors involved in the marriage to help you understand the reasons behind the infidelity and heal from the pain. The majority of serial affair participants are men; although it is possible for a woman to have serial affairs, usually the reasons are different. Serial affair seekers are typically avoiding intimacy in their marriage, so they choose shallow, uncommitted affairs. They toggle back and forth between marriage and mistress because they do not know how to participate in an exclusive, emotionally available relationship (Subotnik & Harris, 2005). In other words, affairs may occur when a man needs to diffuse or evade emotional connection with his spouse (Subotnik & Harris, 2005).

Serial affairs share a common trait with the fling in that there is no emotional commitment with the sexual partner. Having multiple affairs and sexual partners is the antithesis of desiring true intimacy; the opposite of seeking personal closeness with others (Subotnik & Harris, 2005). For example, one woman asked her straying husband if he was in love with his affair partner. He paused and then replied, "There wasn't enough time for romance." Initially she noted feeling relieved that her husband was not in love with another woman. Then she subsequently felt disheartened that he was using another woman for sex. After being educated about the types of affairs, she began to understand that there was no emotional commitment to his affair partner and that he was just acting out his stress in maladaptive and fantasy ways—the affair partner was simply a willing participant.

The straying spouse likely has no intention of leaving the marriage during serial affairs, since the emotional connection to the affair partner is low compared to romantic and long-term affairs to be discussed next. The straying spouse typically has no desire to seek divorce and is content just "getting a little on the side." Despite the lack of emotional investment in the relationship with the sexual partner, the commitment to the marital vow has been breached and compromised (Subotnik & Harris, 2005). Because the betrayed spouse deals with lying and violation of trust repeatedly, the threat to the marriage can be greater compared to the fling. This can happen especially if the pain of discovery occurs on multiple occasions. Marriages can be mended if the straying spouse is willing to demonstrate complete honesty, remorse, and changed behavior over time. Therapy is usually required for healthy relationship repair and trust rejuvenation in this circumstance.

Case Example

Curtis a, thirty-nine-year-old home builder, and Staci, a forty-one-year-old veterinarian, had been married for eleven years, and Curtis had been "fooling around" on his wife for five. In my clinical opinion, he had never experienced real, unconditional, unqualified, love from his family of origin and thus did not know how to give it. Curtis grew up as a child where addiction and mental illness were present, but never addressed. Moreover, his mother had extramarital affairs, so the institution of marriage was not respected within the family system. Staci was unaware of this dynamic when they married. People who witnessed their primary care givers having affairs in their families of origin are more likely to repeat the behaviors because they view them as commonplace (Pittman, 1989). Most important, it was my opinion that Curtis did not receive adequate love as a child, so when he did receive unreserved love in his marriage, he did not know what to do with it or how to reciprocate. He felt inadequate, constantly inferior, and he frequently verbally shamed himself. In therapy, it became clear that Curtis eventually began to secretly reach out to other women in an attempt to fulfill the void within him and avoid closeness with Staci.

Perhaps serial affairs are unhealthy defense mechanisms for low self-esteem, feelings of inadequacy and inferiority, or an inability to achieve a genuine measure of emotional vulnerability necessary for the intimacy required for a meaningful marriage. Straying spouses often attempt to find meaning in irrelevant places. To mitigate feelings of inferiority, straying spouses often establish affairs and "splitting" is the result. Psychological "splitting" occurs when one spouse's energy is divided between two partners. Tim Alan Gardner (2002), author of *Sacred Sex: A Spiritual Celebration of Oneness in Marriage*, noted that most circumstances preceding affairs, including previous traumas, involve some misunderstanding about love, sex, and intimacy. In his 1997 article, *Coping with Infidelity in Marriage*, Dr. Greg Swenson noted that infidelity may be a sign of self-dissatisfaction or a behavioral pattern that seeks self-satisfaction. Feelings of dissatisfaction with self and a sense of entitlement will be discussed later in Chapter 5 in a discussion about underlying personality characteristics that are correlated with infidelity.

Don Juans

Don Juan is the legendary Spanish fictional character set in the 14th century who was known for his numerous sexual liaisons with women and his "love them and leave them" mentality. Dr. Robert Stradling, a professor of history at the University of Wales, is an expert in the account and the legend of Don Juan. Stradling (1993) noted that the playwright Gabriel Tellez, a Spanish priest writing under the pseudonym of Tirso De Molina, originally developed the character Don Juan. Authorities disagree as to the exact date and location of the unveiling of the play, but suggest it was sometime around 1619 and likely in Lisbon, Portugal, where King Phillip III was an attendee (Stradling, 1993). Stradling believed the character of Don Juan was originally modeled after a real life person, Don Juan de Tarsiss y Peralta, Count of Villamediana, who was eventually assassinated. Over generations, the name Don Juan has become synonymous with the word *womanizer*: one who sees a woman as a sexual object, a toy to be played with and then discarded. Don Juan-like behaviors often are characterized by extreme entitlement and sexual exploitation of women. Stradling (1993) noted in his work entitled *The Death of Don Juan: Murder, Myth, and Mayhem in Madrid* that the Don Juan "macho syndrome" maintains a style that "involves the exploitation of women, lifestyles of indolence and conspicuous consumption and notions of honour both vacuous and violent" (p. 11).

Perhaps you know Don Juan better as Don Giovanni, the Italian name, made famous by Wolfgang Amadeus Mozart in his masterpiece opera first performed in Prague in 1787. According to Drs. Peter Reill and Ellen Wilson (2004) in the *Encyclopedia of the Enlightenment*, the libretto for Mozart's opera was written by Lorenzo da Ponte and was entitled *The Libertine Punished, or Don Giovanni.* Webster's Ninth New Collegiate Dictionary defines libertine as "a person who is unrestrained by convention or morality, specifically: one leading a dissolute life." Many authors, artists, musicians, and poets, including the English poet George Gordon Byron, who wrote his epic poem "Don Juan," in 1821, have been fascinated or intrigued by Don Juan's licentious character. Close to one hundred works of art and literature have been written or created since the inception of his character centuries ago to depict his extraordinarily intriguing sexual behavior.

The original play and subsequent opera depict a lothario named Don Juan who engages in multiple sexual encounters with women and then discards them. He happens upon the spirit of the deceased father of one of his women and invites him to dinner. The father accepts, and suggests dinner in the graveyard. Don Juan agrees, and when the ghost reaches out to shake Don Juan's hand, he pulls him into hell.

Interestingly, the story of Don Juan and his notorious womanizing has survived over 390 years, since the first publication occurred in the early 1600s in Spain. Perhaps this indicates that people, cross-culturally and over generations, see serial affairs and sexual objectification as hurtful. Second, the story also suggests that family members, not only women, are impacted and devastated by Don Juan-like behaviors. It is the father of a woman who seeks revenge on Don Juan in the story. The idea that infidelity has far-reaching consequences on the culture and family system beyond the betrayed spouse will be discussed more in detail in Chapter 7. Another important conclusion drawn from the Don Juan story is that in the end of the story Don Juan gets pulled into hell. Most serial affairs don't turn out well. They end up hurting multiple people, including the betrayer and spouse, and almost never lead to healthy relationships with the sexual partner. Serial affairs always cause stress of multiple kinds: financial, interpersonal, legal, and even medical. God intended sex to be experienced exclusively in the marital bed where two become one. There is not room for a third person, for only two can become fused as one according to scripture. Perhaps one reason that the Don Juan label and legend has survived for centuries is because of extensive Christian doctrine that has pervaded our Western belief system about infidelity. In many Eastern or Middle Eastern countries, it is often expected that a married man will have a mistress or two. Perhaps because of the esteemed value and sacredness of marriage described in the Old Testament and the New Testament, and the elevation of the worth of women (mentioned in the New Testament), infidelity is more negatively connoted in the West, which has been shaped by our religious beliefs.

- Therefore shall a man leave his father and his mother, and shall cleave unto his wife: and they shall be one flesh. (Genesis 2:24 KJV)
- Thou shalt not commit adultery. (Exodus 20:14 KJV)
- "You have heard that it was said, 'Do not commit adultery.' But I tell you that anyone who looks at a woman lustfully has already committed adultery with her in his heart . . . " (Matthew 6:27-28 NIV)
- Marriage should be honored by all, and the marriage bed kept pure, for God will judge the adulterer and all the sexually immoral. (Hebrews 13:4 NIV)

Don Juans are the types of philanderers who characteristically engage in serial affairs. Due to its repetitive nature, a serial affair is the type of affair most closely associated with sexual addiction tendencies. Don Juans typically can't stop with a onetime fling, and don't have the emotional capacity to engage in a long-term, more romantic and emotionally invested affair. Don Juans are often charming, personable, likeable, successful individuals, who deep on the inside feel inadequate and insecure, suffering from intense feelings of inferiority.

Sexual Addiction

The Society for the Advancement of Sexual Health (SASH) reported that 3 to 5 percent of Americans experience sexual addiction and compulsivity symptoms. This equates to be over fifteen million people, and SASH noted this is a conservative estimate because they are only reporting numbers of those who seek treatment. In their book *Lonely All the Time: Recognizing, Understanding and Overcoming Sex Addiction, for Addicts and Co-Dependents,* psychologists Dr. Ralph Earle and Dr. Gregory Crow (1989) noted that most sex addicts share the common trait of coming from a family of origin where physical, emotional, or sexual abuse by a parent occurred; or, a parent was addicted or displayed compulsive tendencies. This suggests some of the environmental shaping of the origin of addiction. Some people may develop addictive behavioral patterns out of protective measures to shield themselves from abuse or out of habit because of poor role-modeling of parents. Earle and Crow (1989) described five common "seeds" of addiction that are noteworthy of mentioning:

- a tendency to hold low opinions of themselves and to constantly remind themselves of their deficiencies
- distorted or unrealistic beliefs about themselves, their behavior, other people, and the events that occur in the world around them
- a desire to escape from or to suppress unpleasant emotions
- difficulty coping with stress; at least one powerful memory of an intense high experienced at a crucial time in their lives and an ever-present desire to recapture the euphoric feeling
- an uncanny ability to deny that they have a problem (p. 28).

Other behaviors to assess in individuals to determine if sexual addiction is present include:

- Loss of control of sexual behaviors or impulses
- Compulsive or ritualistic sexual behaviors
- Viewing pornography
- Sexual objectification of partners
- Attending sexually oriented businesses (strip clubs, adult video, etc.)
- Efforts, often unsuccessful, to cease the sexual acting out

- Loss of time
- Preoccupation with thinking about sex
- Inability to fulfill routine obligations (work, marital, family, parenting, financial, etc.)
- Continuation of unhealthy sexual behaviors despite negative consequences
- Escalation of sexual behaviors
- Losses (divorce, loss of job, friends, financial resources)
- Social withdrawal
- Lack of concern regarding their behavioral impact on others
- Feelings of guilt and shame
- Unsafe or risky sexual behaviors
- Prostitution
- Participating in cybersex or phone sex
- Sexual aversion
- Co-morbidity with other addictions (alcohol, drug addictions)

Not only is there evidence of environmental factors influencing the development of addictions, but biology perhaps plays a role as well. Scientists have also determined that individuals with sex addictions have brain chemistries similar to those with other addictive disorders, like alcoholism or drug dependency. Whether these specific brain chemistries are the cause of addiction or are shaped by an unhealthy social environment has been an age old question. Perhaps the answer lies in a complex combination of nature and nurture. Sexual addiction, as noted above, often coexists with other addictions.

Treatment of Sexual Addiction

The treatment focus for sexual addiction is the comprehensive medical model that includes the 12-step program (inpatient or outpatient), individual therapy (couples and family if necessary), and medication management if a concurring mental health issue is present. Changes in friendships and environment (changes in playmates and play places) are often an important part of recovery. Healthy people who value sexual sobriety are sought out as friends and support after recovery to help the newly sober addict maintain monogamy.

Accountability groups and support groups like Sex and Love Addicts Anonymous (SLAA), as well as aftercare groups following formal treatment, are essential to maintaining sobriety. SLAA is an international 12-step recovery organization that assists people in maintaining sobriety from sex or love addictions. Further information can be accessed from their website at slaafws.org.

Moreover, individual therapy is a significant and integral part of the individual's treatment, because recovery will be a lifelong journey and individual therapy aids in insight enhancement, behavioral change, coping skill development, and relapse prevention. Additionally, individual therapy aids in facilitating complete and total honesty which is necessary for psychological growth, addiction recovery, and shame reduction for the person with sexual addiction. Furthermore, it helps the individual take accountability for his sexual behaviors and to amend and repair damaged relationships for which he is responsible. Most treatment programs include a family program where spouses or family members can participate because addiction is a "family" disease in that it impacts the entire family system. If your spouse has a sexual addiction and decides to seek treatment, make sure to ask about the family program, for this can be an essential part of your education and healing.

Pornography

Pornography is a curse to the marital relationship. It never leads to greater levels of love, intimacy, trust, or companionship in a marriage. In my counseling practice, I have never seen beneficial results when individuals or couples view pornography in an attempt to enhance their sexual relationship. In fact, viewing pornography seemed to increase the levels of distrust and fear in the marital relationship.

Through each encounter with pornography, the individual attempts to seek sexual satisfaction from an artificial object or relationship. The pornography viewer deludes himself into thinking the relationship is real and he finds himself needing more frequent encounters to satisfy arousal because his tolerance has increased and the pleasure is temporary.

Pornography is incompatible with love. Pornography sexually objectifies women and children and undermines the sacredness of sexual "oneness" between husband and wife. Pornography can never replace sexual and emotional intimacy with your spouse. Pornography involves a third party in the sexual relationship and therefore it is incompatible with God's design, which was for two fleshes to become one. "The man said, 'This is now bone of my bones and flesh of my flesh; she shall be called woman, for she was taken out of man'" (Genesis 2:23 NIV).

Pornography can be a "gateway" behavior that often leads to feelings of shame, sexual addiction, or affairs. Pornography undermines the integrity of the sacredness of the marriage. Gardner (2002) describes pornography as a "deadly intrusion" that must be battled with prayer and love.

Differential Diagnosis: Mental Health Disorders

Certain sexual addiction symptoms or affair behaviors may mimic particular mental health symptoms of other disorders. It is important, especially with serial affairs, to determine if the straying spouse has a co-morbid mental health condition. For example, manic or hypo-manic symptoms of Bipolar Disorder are often characterized by sexual impulsivity or hypersexuality. Other disorders, such as Schizoaffective Disorder, Obsessive Compulsive Disorder, or Substance Induced Mood Disorders can also present with sexual impulsivity.

Case Example

Kevin came to my office for individual therapy following a brief inpatient hospital stay for Bipolar Disorder, his most recent episode manic. He was in his early thirties and had had multiple sexual indiscretions, frequenting swingers' clubs, having meaningless, impulsive one night stands, etc., throughout his eight year marriage. After his official Bipolar diagnosis, we discovered retrospectively that his affairs occurred during his unmedicated manic episodes. With his commitment to ongoing medication management and an accountability plan in therapy, he was able to maintain a faithful commitment to his marriage for the remainder of his treatment.

Obsessive Compulsive Disorder

Obsessive Compulsive Disorder (OCD) is also important to assess because some obsessions and compulsions can be sexual in their presentation. Obsessions (intrusive and repetitive thoughts) and compulsions (impulsive and compelling acting out of the thoughts) can be sexual and ritualistic in nature. If you believe your spouse could have this mental health condition, it is important that he or she be evaluated by a professional. OCD symptoms can be manifested in sexually pathological ways (i.e., obsessing over a sexual fantasy until it is completed, engaging in particular and specific masturbatory rituals, or homophobic contamination fears). OCD symptoms, although not necessarily an infringement upon marital vows, can be mistaken by spouses as indications of infidelity due to changes in sexual behaviors and sexual routines. Nevertheless, the behaviors can often be disturbing or troubling to the patient, as well as to the marital and sexual relationship, and thus need to be addressed by a professional. Understanding OCD can make a big difference in the healing process for the betrayed spouse when infidelity is an issue. Therapies and medications can be very helpful in understanding and managing symptoms. OCD patients should arm themselves with the triad of education, therapy, and medication.

Romantic Affairs

Romantic affairs are characterized by more emotional investment with the affair partner than flings or serial affairs. Straying spouses erroneously believe that the romance is real and better than the current marriage and often glorify and sensationalize the relationship. Romantic affair partners are so often caught up in the irrational feelings of the affair that they feel compelled to decide whether to end the affair or leave their marriage and marry their lover (Subotnik & Harris, 2005).

For example, Josh, a banker in his mid-thirties, shared with me that one of his young lovers wanted him to leave his wife and "run away with her to France to be married," despite the fact that she was engaged to another man and he was married with three young children. Partners in romantic affairs are often preoccupied with incorporating the affair into their lives (Subotnik & Harris, 2005). The clandestine and novel nature of the romantic affair often makes it tantalizing to the straying spouse and adds to the irrational belief system that the romantic feelings are pure and real. The lie of infidelity perpetuates the distorted view that the straying spouse's needs will be fulfilled by a lover.

Some romantic affairs do turn into long-term affairs. What the straying spouse does not realize is that the romantic affair is originating out of secrecy and mistrust and this prohibits likeliness of a long-term, healthy, monogamous, trusting relationship being sustained. Staheli

(1995) reported that fewer than 10 percent of relationships that begin from an extramarital affair will actually result in a marriage between the two affair partners. Of those that do, 75 percent will end in divorce. Pittman (1989) similarly noted that, "Throughout all cultures, in all great literature, infidelity is rarely rewarded" (p. 29).

Case Example

For example, Anne came to my office for therapy. She had been having a long distance affair for eight months. She had reconnected with an old college boyfriend via e-mail and they had met on half a dozen occasions in a neighboring city three hours away. She was mesmerized with him and called him her "soul mate." She cooed that they were destined to be together and it was "so right this time." They should never have broken up in college. Anne had a full time job as an account executive for a major marketing firm in town and had three children in elementary school. Her lover, three hours away, had two children from his first marriage, two from his second, and was a pediatrician with a thriving practice and no plans of moving to the Dallas area. Anne loved her job and didn't want to uproot her children, especially her middle child, who suffered from Down's Syndrome and was in a special needs program in the school district. Despite all the barriers that seemed obvious to me, Anne insisted on making spreadsheets calculating financial budgets about joint household incomes for this would-be family of nine. It wasn't until the affair was discovered by the doctor's wife that the relationship between Anne and her lover was terminated. It was only after causing much pain for both betrayed spouses and trouble for the children that she was able to see her fantastical thoughts and irrationality.

Long-Term Affairs

Long-term affairs are clandestine relationships that last years, and sometimes decades, of time. Long-term affairs can originate from flings, romantic affairs, or reconnections with former lovers. For example, Michelle learned that her husband of forty-three years had been having an affair over the course of thirty years of their marriage. This was a shocking blow to her and her adult children. The discovery of a long-term affair can be emotionally devastating to the betrayed spouse. Long-term affairs pose the greatest risk to the integrity of the marriage and the emotional investment with the affair partner is high given the length of time of involvement. Subotnik and Harris (2005) described long-term affairs as "formidable" (p. 13).

Take the case of Gretchen, who learned that her husband of twenty-three years had been having an affair with the next door neighbor for five years. He disclosed his affair while they were waiting on the birth of twin grandchildren. Her husband decided to leave the marriage in order to marry his affair partner. Although most affairs do not develop into healthy, trust-centered, monogamous relationships, sometimes straying spouses divorce and marry the affair partner. As cited previously, most statistics are grim for the health and stability for affair induced relationships. Most affair-born relationships do not last because they are damaged from the beginning and based upon dishonesty, secrecy, unrealistic expectations, underdeveloped trust, and a fantasy or "vacation-like" relationship experience. Realistically, affair participants should question one another's ability to form a relationship derived from infidelity.

Is Male Monogamy Biological?

Despite it being socially desirable, monogamy, and more broadly, trustworthiness, is never guaranteed in any human relationship. Scientists have researched the mating processes of many species, both animal and human, and have found some to be monogamous and some to be promiscuous. Louann Brizendine (2010), author of *The Male Brain: A Breakthrough Understanding of How Men and Boys Think*, suggested that understanding the primitive sexual genetics of voles (a mouse-like rodent) could be a link to understanding the monogamous versus promiscuous nature of man. She reported that two chemicals are released during male mating habits: dopamine and vasopressin. Much like voles, human brains also have vasopressin receptor sites that are stimulated during the sexual mating process, although the human brain is much more complex than a rodent's.

Brizendine (2010) reported that prairie voles have longer vasopressin receptor genes and their cousins, the montane voles, have a shorter form of the vasopressin receptor gene. Subsequently, the prairie vole is a monogamous creature and the montane vole demonstrates promiscuous sexual mating habits. It appears that a longer version of the vasopressin receptor gene is associated with monogamous sexual mating behaviors and shorter genes are connected with having multiple sexual partners (Brizendine, 2010).

Is this revolutionary information we can use for our understanding of human relationships? Are men with longer vasopressin receptor genes able to maintain monogamous relationships more frequently? Brizendine (2010) noted a Swiss study found that men who had longer vasopressin receptor genes were two times as likely to leave singlehood and commit for a lifetime to a woman. She reported, "So when it comes to fidelity, the joke among female scientists is that 'longer is better,' at least when it comes to the length of the vasopressin receptor gene" (Brizendine, 2010, p. 60).

Discussion Questions

1. What type(s) of affair(s) did your straying partner have?
2. How does identifying the type of affair your partner engaged in help in your healing journey?
3. Do you believe that the level of pain is different for different types of affairs?
4. Do you believe that certain types of affairs are easier to recover from?
5. Was sexual addiction or pornography a problem in your marriage? What did you do to cope?

CHAPTER 5

NARCISSISM

In this section, I will discuss a brief overview of Narcissistic Personality Disorder (NPD), its diagnostic criteria, and its relationship to infidelity. I will explore each symptom individually and give clinical examples. Understanding whether your spouse has NPD can help you identify specific pathological symptoms, understand problematic behaviors, and change your responses and reactions. Knowledge will enable you to cope with the narcissistic tendencies of your spouse and stop personalizing the negative impact of the narcissist's behaviors.

Are people with certain personality traits more likely to commit adultery? Todd Shackelford and David Buss researched over one hundred characteristics of personality to determine precursors to infidelity. They found three traits that were correlated with higher incidences of infidelity: narcissism, low conscientiousness, and psychoticism. Low conscientiousness was defined by Buss (2000) as individuals who demonstrated unreliable, negligent, careless, and disorganized behaviors. Other behavioral characteristics displayed were laziness, impulsivity, and lack of self-control. Psychoticism is not as it sounds, for the actual psychiatric definition of psychosis is to have hallucinations or delusions, and this is different than Buss' definition. The psychoticism dimension he studied was similar to behaviors of low conscientiousness and narcissism. Impulsivity and lack of inhibitory control (associated with low conscientiousness), manipulative behavior, interpersonal exploitation, and lack of empathy were characteristics associated with a narcissism diagnosis (Buss, 2000). Narcissism will be the focus of this section.

NPD is a pervasive, destructive disorder that impacts all areas of functioning: interpersonal, occupational, and social. Although personality disorders cannot be officially diagnosed until one reaches adulthood (because the personality is still formulating), narcissistic personality traits begin developing and revealing themselves as early as childhood.

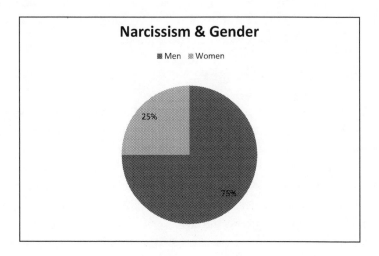

According to the *Diagnostic and Statistical Manual of Mental Disorders TR-IV*, NPD is widely gender specific, with 75 percent of those diagnosed being male. Because the majority of individuals with narcissism are men, I will use the male pronoun "he" for the purposes of this discussion. The prognosis of individuals with NPD will be discussed in the next section.

Prognosis

Narcissism's prognosis is typically poor. Dr. Sam Vaknin (2008), author of *Malignant Self Love: Narcissism Revisited*, postulated that several reasons exist for the narcissist's poor prognosis. First is his great tendency to deny reality. Second, when a narcissist attends therapy, it is often a "useless" or "tedious" experience for both patient and therapist because behavior change is unlikely. The narcissist's behavioral patterns rarely change because his thinking archetypes are so deeply ingrained with distortions of reality (Vaknin, 2008). Third, Vaknin (2008) reported that narcissists participate in pathological lying. Whether they believe their lies or justify them, their dishonesty is part of their pathology. Since honesty and transparency are necessary for growth, insight, and maturation, lying prohibits the narcissist from making progress. Also, Vaknin (2008) noted that narcissism has become adaptive (although maladaptive) for the individual. The narcissist has developed behaviors over years, sometimes decades, to protect himself from hurt, fear, shame, ridicule, abuse, criticism, or other ego threats. His maladaptive tendencies have become reinforced over time and served purposes to protect him. How do these tendencies develop?

Foundations of Narcissism

An individual with narcissism fears inferiority or unconsciously believes that he is inferior. When asked, he would project aloud that he is superior, for to admit inferiority would be the ultimate shame and a sign of weakness. A patient in my office claimed to have "high self-esteem" out loud; however, after a therapy session, he would examine himself in the mirror above my couch and mutter to himself how fat and ugly he was and berate himself about his size.

The narcissist's defense mechanisms short-circuit the capacity to allow shame into his experience or the ability to acknowledge his feared inadequacy. Whereas the egocentric behavioral patterns may have once served a useful purpose in childhood, say, to protect him from a verbally abusive mother, they are no longer effective and are quite destructive in his adult life, wreaking havoc in his job or marriage. Individuals with narcissism are perplexed as to why they keep having one relationship end after another or why repeated job failures or dissatisfactions occur. Behaviors that were adaptive and necessary in childhood no longer work when honesty, empathy, and generosity are needed in the real world to have relationship and occupational sustainability. To request him to change these belief systems is an anathema to him, for it is all he has ever known and would suggest that he is flawed.

An individual with narcissism is suspect of people in general, because of his experience in his family of origin. He is always questioning whether his mother would be present and kind, or cruel and abandoning. Perhaps he developed a pseudo-self-sufficiency out of a necessity to protect himself so as not to need her. He could not depend on her because of her lack of consistency. In other words, it was too painful to risk trusting her; for it was easier to distance himself from her, count on himself, and believe he was special and entitled.

Sometimes the unhealthy parent reinforced the child's emerging narcissistic defense mechanisms out of his or her own guilt about being harsh and abandoning. To compensate for poor parenting, the child is lavished with indulgent compliments and unrealistic adulation. This confuses the child about his identity, thereby reinforcing the narcissistic tendencies of specialness and grandiosity.

Other individuals with narcissistic traits received excessive admiration and adoration from overindulgent parents—parents with good intentions who inadvertently created monsters. Too much indulgence and praise without realistic feedback and necessary discipline can be damaging to the child's development.

The narcissist began to act out in childhood with defense mechanisms including cutting in line, having difficulty sharing toys, and exploiting others to reinforce his egotistical façade that he was superior. He was always craving compliments, needing more of them to buttress his self-image. This hunger sometimes led to the charming behaviors exhibited by a narcissist when he attempts to win others' love and approval. Layer upon layer and year after year, these thought patterns and needs were established. When someone challenged him or did not appease him, he blamed or criticized them so as not to have to break his adaptations. It would be too painful to look within himself or think he might have to adjust to a social or cultural norm and be considered "ordinary."

An individual with narcissism has come to distrust people, sometimes being pathologically paranoid, or alternatively sees himself as blazingly superior to others. Relationships with people have been superficial, a means to an end only to achieve what he wants. Individuals with narcissism wildly seek out others, but often only to fulfill their own needs, achieve self-aggrandizement, or to pretend that they are playing the part that society expects of them. For example, a man may take a wife and desire to have a family to appease cultural expectations, all the while having mistresses on the side, exploiting his wife and other women along the way. The specific symptoms of NPD will be discussed in the following section.

Specific Symptoms of Narcissism

There are nine symptoms of NPD according to *The Diagnostic and Statistical Manual of Manual of Mental Disorders TR-IV* (p. 717):

- Has a grandiose sense of self-importance (e.g., exaggerates achievements and talents, expects to be recognized as superior without commensurate achievements)

- Is preoccupied with fantasies of unlimited success, power, brilliance, beauty, or ideal love
- Believes that he or she is "special" or unique and can only be understood by, or should associate with, other special or high-status people (or institutions)
- Requires excessive admiration
- Has a sense of entitlement, i.e., unreasonable expectations of especially favorable treatment or automatic compliance with his or her expectations
- Is interpersonally exploitive, i.e., takes advantage of others to achieve his or her own ends
- Lacks empathy: is unwilling to recognize or identify with the feelings and needs of others
- Is often envious of others or believes others are envious of him or her
- Shows arrogant, haughty behaviors or attitudes

To be diagnosed, one must meet five of the nine symptoms. Therefore, this leads to a variety of presentations of NPD, because not all individuals with narcissism share the same symptom set. In other words, one narcissist may look very different from another narcissist. For example, one individual may present with envy, arrogant and haughty behaviors and another individual may not. It is important to familiarize yourself with all of the symptoms when trying to understand if your loved one meets the criteria for the disorder. In the next section, I will individually explore all of the nine symptoms and their relationship to infidelity.

Individual Symptoms Explored

Grandiose Sense of Self-Importance

Narcissists have grandiose thoughts that they are superior to others; that they should be automatically important whether or not they have put the work in to merit favor, achievement, or honor. Narcissists love to share their accomplishments, whether real, fabricated, or embellished; dishonesty is not a deterrent. Upon initially meeting new people, narcissists eagerly share their achievements, usually exaggerated, to boost their egos and to stabilize their position with their new acquaintance. I once had a patient who, during the first session, told me four times how much money he made. Conversely, a patient I was encouraging to open up and reveal more of himself had a mistaken belief and fear that "sharing more about himself with others would be boasting." His distorted belief, although not healthy, let me know he was definitely *not* a narcissist.

The grandiose sense of self-importance can be troubling to a relationship because the one exhibiting narcissistic tendencies is typically focused on himself and not on his spouse or the betterment or enrichment of the marriage. If the narcissist is giving to the spouse, it is often to achieve his own means of being admired or placating the spouse temporarily to meet his own needs. For example, one man would bring coffee to his wife each morning and then ask her, "Aren't you going to tell me how great I am for bringing you coffee?" He wasn't bringing coffee to her to be generous or to give her an unreserved gift; his intention was to get narcissistic admiration by bringing her a cup of coffee. This is what Vaknin (2008) labels "narcissistic supply." The individual with narcissism must continually hunt for ways to fill his innermost void—his narcissistic supply—with words of adulation, sexual conquests, achievements, associations with perceived high-status individuals, etc. Out of desperation, some narcissists turn to destructive avenues of seeking narcissistic supply, including pornography, sex with prostitutes, affairs, alcohol, drugs, gambling, or some combination of these behaviors. This is where this symptom of grandiose sense of self-importance can be connected to infidelity. If the narcissist's narcissistic supply is low, he may turn to sex with another individual outside his marriage to fill him up. Because he believes he is more important than others (i.e., his spouse and the marriage), he does not think that he is subject to following the rules that other people value, like commitments or vows. He is above those things because of his perceived level of importance.

Preoccupation with Fantasies of Unlimited Success, Power, Brilliance, Beauty, or Ideal Love

People with narcissism are often very intelligent, successful, and charming individuals. This is what can make them so attractive and perplexing, yet many of them lead such secret, duplicitous, and tortured lives. Narcissists are typically on a tireless mission to prove themselves to others and to defend themselves against the enemies of shame and inferiority. Individuals with narcissism can become obsessed with an idea or a fantasy; healthy or unhealthy, realistic or unrealistic. They become fixated and spend hours of time, energy, and even money on making the fantasy become a reality. This obsession can be destructive to a relationship if the fantasy is not shared by a spouse or is an unhealthy, grandiose, unrealistic, or destructive fantasy. Some individuals desire to have so much power that they are feared by others. This allows them to avoid emotional closeness and prevent interpersonal intimacy; perceptions which could lead to exposure of weakness. They enjoy being feared or hated and capitalize on intimidating others with their power. Those obsessed with power or winning cannot even tolerate losing at cards or a board game. One female patient complained to me that her husband would rage with anger and then brood for hours if he lost at checkers. One time she reported he threw cards across the table and refused to speak to friends for days when he lost at a game of bridge. Other narcissists obsess about ideal romance in relationships and desire their wives to be "perfect" sexually and in appearance like in the movies or advertisements. One man excessively obsessed about his wife's weight gain to the point where he developed sexual dysfunction. He threatened to divorce her if she did not lose thirteen pounds. He blamed his dysfunction on her and told her the only way he would stay married to her was if she got liposuction. These expectations are unrealistic and damaging to the wife's self-esteem and to the integrity of the marriage. These narcissists see women as sexual objects and their obsessions are distortions. These men are especially susceptible to viewing pornography and engaging in extramarital affairs.

Belief of Specialness

Similar to a grandiose sense of self-importance, narcissists believe that they are special and irreplaceable. Moreover, they erroneously believe that they can only connect with and be understood by people of high status. One man asked his wife, who had a neurological condition that presented itself by stuttering, if she felt dependent on him in the marriage. He stated that "no one would want you because of your stuttering." He felt so superior, matchless, and special and viewed her as dependent, delinquent, and damaged because of her speech impediment. It was only later that his wife learned he had participated in several extramarital affairs. Another example was a man who only chose to interact with people of his race and economic status. He looked down upon others whom he deemed less worthy than him and evaluated prospective friends and clients based on their income level or potential, whether or not they attended an "acceptable school," and what they could offer him.

This symptom of specialness is a denial of reality and impacts relationships by creating an inequality between the two partners, with the narcissist believing he is superior and his partner inferior. It is a denial of reality because, truth be told, all of us are special, uniquely created by God, making none of us special in a "superior" sense. We are all ordinary human beings trying to live and survive life. We are all made of DNA, all the same species, all created in God's image. There is no scripture that says certain human beings are superior to others. God said, " . . . thou shalt love thy neighbor as thyself" (Leviticus 19:18 KJV). The narcissist's belief in his own specialness sets up a power differential that leads to abuse and mistreatment by the narcissist. This belief in his own specialness, makes him susceptible to discarding vows and discrediting others' feelings. The person with narcissistic tendencies is more likely than others without the diagnosis to believe he is so special that he should have whatever he wants, even at the expense of others; therefore, this makes him more vulnerable to infidelity. Furthermore, Vaknin (2008) reported that monogamous marriages and raising children are behaviors common in ordinary people, and the narcissist feels cheated by the ordinariness of these mundane institutions. Being a husband and a father reduces the individual with narcissism to being average, and this perceived psychological wound leads him to choose affairs to boost his superiority and sense of specialness (Vaknin, 2008).

Need for Excessive Admiration

Individuals with narcissism crave repetitive admiration and adulation. One narcissist asked his wife, "Have you told me that you love me today?" The wife frustratingly replied, "Yes, honey, I told you for the sixth time five minutes ago." How easily the narcissist forgets, for the words do not have permanence for him. The compliments and words of admiration wear off and are only temporary. He finds himself famished and needy for validation again. It is as if the individual with narcissism has a hole in his heart that needs to be relentlessly filled with reassurance that he is acceptable. This need can become draining and exhausting for the one in the relationship with an insatiable narcissist. Take, for example, this conversation from a therapy session:

Bill: "I just want to be told I do a good job."

Katherine: "I do think you do a good job."

Bill: "That is not enough from you. I want to be told I do a great job!"

Katherine: "I just told you I think you do a good job, which is what you originally asked for and now I am being penalized for it."

If the narcissist does not feel like the spouse is doing a sufficient job admiring him, he may seek adulation and adoration outside the marriage. Because the narcissist's needs for worship are so profound and his expectations are unrealistic and excessively demanding, it is unlikely that he will ever be satisfied in a monogamous relationship. This puts him in danger of seeking solace outside the marriage in affairs and places his partner at risk of being betrayed and emotionally wounded.

Sense of Entitlement

Individuals displaying narcissism have a sense of entitlement and expect especially favorable treatment. Moreover, they have unreasonable expectations of others and demand automatic compliance with their expectations or they often go into a rage of anger. The narcissist hates rules, particularly those that limit his pleasure, unless they stifle his opponent and allow for personal success. Narcissists believe they are above social mores and norms. It is not unusual to see a narcissist cut in line, misuse professional credentials for personal profit, cross boundaries clearly marked "Do Not Enter," or "Employees Only," or bribe restaurant attendants to be seated more quickly while others patiently wait their turn. The rules and conventions of society apply to "everyone else," or so the narcissist mistakenly thinks.

Because narcissists feel they are entitled to have their needs met, they believe that their demands should be fulfilled immediately and without question. They do not understand that others have the right to delay or even decline their requests.

A sense of entitlement can be a precursor to infidelity because the narcissist may feel "entitled" to have whatever he wants, including relationships on the side. Monogamous relationships require sacrifice, empathy, and generous, selfless giving, which are qualities antithetical to entitlement. Vaknin (2008) noted that a narcissist interprets the reciprocal necessity of "give and take" in a healthy relationship as a threat and is more likely to seek outside relationships to recapture a feeling of perceived control. The sense of entitlement is an obstacle to healthy relationships and can be a warning sign for infidelity.

Interpersonal Exploitation

Narcissists use other people to achieve their own purposes. The narcissist does not think about the consequences of hurting other people; he is merely concerned with boosting his own narcissistic supply. Narcissists may use friendships to their advantage without reciprocating and seldom think about giving without getting something in return. When others lovingly give to narcissists, they expect it because of their beliefs of specialness and entitlement. Alternatively, the narcissist may question the person giving, suspicious of an ulterior motive.

Narcissists exploit other people by using them for their talents, their wealth, or their services. The narcissist rarely offers his own services unless he is looking for verbal validation and recognition to fuel his narcissistic supply. A severe case of exploitation would be a narcissist using a woman for sex with no intention of establishing a relationship with her. The woman is left feeling rejected and used, while the narcissist has his ego boosted by another sexual conquest. One man reported to me that he would go out in the evening to seek one night stands with other women while his wife was at home. This is an example of exploitation of women, using them as sexual objects, playing with them as if they were toys. The narcissist then discards them after his personal needs have been met, all the while disrespecting the marital boundaries. Vaknin (2008) wrote:

The narcissist objectifies people and treats them as expendable commodities to be discarded after use . . . Yet, it is the mechanical, thoughtless, heartless, face of narcissistic abuse—devoid of human passions and of familiar emotions—that renders it so alien, so frightful and so repellent (p. 305).

We can see why exploitation of others would be a warning sign for infidelity, since individuals with narcissism care less about the welfare of others or relationships than their own personal gain.

Lack of Empathy

Narcissists have difficulty expressing empathy and unqualified concern for others. They have trouble stepping outside of their anxious, disturbed, and self-absorbed lives to imagine the unique experience of what things might be like for someone else. Since empathy is a necessary and essential condition for healthy relationships, narcissists have difficulty maintaining long-term, intimate, stable interpersonal relationships. Individuals in relationships with narcissists may eventually find themselves feeling deceived or betrayed. The narcissist may have initially presented or pretended to be loving, caring, and attentive in the relationship, but only for the means of courtship or landing the relationship. Once again, his motive is to fulfill his narcissistic supply. The narcissist's allure, charm, and personable nature can be very attractive to unassuming partners who are not expecting deception, duplicity, or an absence of empathy.

Narcissists are unable to hear their partners' concerns, no matter how many times they are told. One man's wife complained of hurt feelings when her husband would flirt and make sexual comments to his ex-wife in front of her. He continued the behavior despite her repeated requests that he stop. Another husband groped his wife's breasts in public for years despite her continued protests that it made her feel cheap. One can see that the lack of empathy disregards the feelings of others. In the two aforementioned examples, each man was sexually disrespecting his wife and disregarding her sexual feelings. These behaviors eventually evolved into more serious sexual transgressions of infidelity. Thus, lack of empathy, generally defined as a disregard for the feelings of others, can be an antecedent to infidelity.

Envy

Narcissists are often envious of others or distortedly believe that others are envious of them. Narcissists have difficulty celebrating the joys and successes of others. Never content when others have triumph, they often delight in others' misfortunes. Because of their own unconscious dissatisfaction with themselves they envy the success of others. To celebrate in the joy or achievement of another would be empathic and this is an anathema to a narcissist and counterproductive to fulfilling the narcissistic supply. For example, one man explained how he would ridicule his friends and laugh at their mistakes to make himself feel superior. On the other hand, he would become more depressed and mope if his coworker received an accolade at work and he did not.

Narcissists may believe that others envy them. Perhaps this is because they believe they are special and they erroneously think others see them as such. Moreover, narcissists project their envying tendency on others. In other words, *"If I think enviously, others must think enviously."* This line of thinking is distorted and dichotomous and evidences a lack of empathy. It does not consider the fact that just because one envies, another may not.

Regarding infidelity, narcissists may be more susceptible to adulterous relationships because they envy what others have. A narcissist may envy or covet another man's wife, girlfriend, or be jealous of the freedom of a single friend's lifestyle. Feeling envious breeds discontent with oneself and could cause one to be more apt to stray from one's marriage. scripture warns "A heart at peace gives life to the body, but envy rots the bones" (Proverbs 14:30 NIV).

Arrogant and Haughty Behaviors and Attitudes

Narcissists have a tendency to be egotistical, conceited, patronizing, and contemptuous. They can be verbally critical and can churn out sharp put downs. They are quick to blame others to avoid the possibility of looking within themselves, for that would be too anxiety producing to consider self-exploration. Narcissists are less likely to use praise and give compliments unless it is to serve the purpose of making them look good in the eyes of others. Narcissists think they are the best, above reproach. If confronted about breaking a rule, they will demonstrate arrogant and angry behaviors. For example, one man, a security guard by profession, when caught attempting to smuggle extra bottles of alcohol across the border, responded with arrogance and intimidation to the customs agent. He told the agent, "I am in charge." On subsequent trips, the man continued to attempt to smuggle alcohol across the border. He was sometimes caught and had the alcohol confiscated, and at other times successful, determined to be above the rules.

Regarding infidelity, narcissists who are arrogant and believe they are above the rules, do not care about vows or commitments. They do not believe the rules apply to them or will rationalize how, in any instance, they are the "exception" to the rules. Vows made before a community, at church, and before God do not pertain to them because they are special and unique and not subject to such commitments, no matter how sacred. This leads the narcissist to being exceptionally vulnerable to the lure of infidelity.

What to Do if You Are Married to a Narcissist

It is beyond the scope of this book to thoroughly answer the important question *"What do I do if I am married to a narcissist?"* However, I will share two pieces of essential wisdom to explore: therapy and education. First, if you think you might be married to a narcissist, it will be important to seek therapy so you can gain insight into yourself and understand the relationship dynamics between you and the narcissist. The non-narcissist spouse can learn healthy ways of responding to narcissistic behaviors so as to minimize enabling narcissistic symptoms. The narcissist must learn to derive his own happiness and personal satisfaction, and not rely on others or external sources to meet his ego needs. Second, educate yourself about the symptoms of narcissism, for, as I have said, knowledge is empowering. A great resource for understanding more about narcissism is *Malignant Self-Love: Narcissism Revisited* by Dr. Sam Vaknin, which can be found in the reference section of this book.

Discussion Questions

1. Do you think your partner has narcissistic tendencies?
2. What specific symptoms of NPD do you find most difficult to tolerate?
3. Do you believe that narcissistic characteristics played a role in you or your partner's choice to have an affair?

CHAPTER 6

DISCOVERY

Discovery of a mate's affair is the beginning of an arduous journey of pain and suffering that can eventually lead to healing. In addition to forgiveness, specific techniques to help you nurture yourself and eventually heal will be discussed in Chapter 10. Discovery can be a long-term process of encountering clues and warning signs of infidelity along the way. Contrarily, some are indoctrinated into the world of adultery through immediate shock and surprise. Retrospective insight is always more clear to us when evaluating our marriages. It is much easier to look back on the relationship with knowledge of the affair(s) and deduce inconsistencies or behaviors of significance.

In many situations, unassuming spouses finally discover an indisputable sign of infidelity, despite affairs taking place for years before that. It is easy to blame and criticize yourself saying you *should* have seen the signs. Betrayed spouses must be careful of their own self-talk and make sure it is not evaluative or critical with imperatives of what they *should* have done or *could* have done. One betrayed spouse, a social worker in the mental health community, had the mistaken belief that, *"Surely, my clinical training would have prepared me to see the warning signs."* I encourage you to replace criticism and condemnation with compassion. Many fear judgment from others. Another betrayed woman noted that she was fearful others would judge her for choosing a dishonest, unfaithful partner. She had chided herself, saying *"I should have seen it coming,"* since infidelity had occurred in two of her marriages. Another common pitfall is being concerned about what others are thinking. This is an example of negative self-talk, specifically mindreading, and will only delay your healing time. Although it is human to wonder what others are thinking, being overly concerned with others' thoughts can be consuming and exhausting. In the case of infidelity, we are often concerned about what others will think once the secret of an affair is exposed. Traditionally, most people are compassionate toward betrayed spouses. However, if they are not, what they think is not helpful and should be discarded.

What I have come to understand about affairs, is that they are born out of secrecy, duplicity, and lies. True love is meant to be cherished and publically celebrated and never originates from secrecy, falsehood, or disguise. The straying partner becomes an expert in foolery, building story upon story, manipulating the truth, regardless of the irrationality and disparity of truth. When you believe in love and fundamentally trust your partner, you don't think to look for inconsistencies in his behavior or you are quick to dismiss the discrepancies with benign alternative explanations. In other words, the idea of infidelity can be so foreign to the betrayed spouse that the power of love is projected as protectiveness and denial when initial warning signs of infidelity are displayed.

Case Example of Discovery

Amanda, a forty-six-year-old freelance writer, found her first definitive and disturbing clue of her husband's infidelity by finding condoms in his briefcase. Prior to confronting him, she prayed fervently, hoping there was some logical explanation for her troubling discovery. She was desperate for benign answers to a finding that she knew deep down inside meant something dreadful. When you are anxious, turn to the Lord in prayer. Make any and all requests to the Lord and know that He delights in hearing from His children. No prayer is ever unworthy. We may not always get the answer we want when we pray to God, but we do get a promise that God hears every prayer and loves us unconditionally and dearly. In fact, He loves us so much that He reserves a special vessel for our treasured prayers—He collects them and keeps them in a bowl of precious gold, a scriptural word picture illustrating how important our prayers are to God. Similarly, it is written, "Record my lament; list my tears on your scroll—are they not in your record?" (Psalm 56:8 NIV)

- And when he had taken it, the four living creatures and the twenty-four elders fell down before the Lamb. Each one had a harp and they were holding golden bowls full of incense, which are the prayers of the saints. Revelation 5:8 (NIV)

- And pray in the spirit on all occasions with all kinds of prayers and requests. With this in mind, be alert and always keep on praying for all the saints. Ephesians 6:18 (NIV)
- I urge, then, first of all, that requests, prayers, intercession and thanksgiving be made for everyone—for kings and all those in authority, that we may live peaceful and quiet lives in all godliness and holiness. I Timothy 2:1-2 (NIV)
- The priests and the Levites stood to bless the people, and God heard them, for their prayer reached heaven, his holy dwelling place. II Chronicles 30:27 (NIV)
- Do not be anxious about anything, but in everything, by prayer and petition, with thanksgiving, present your requests to God. Philippians 4:6 (NIV)

If you have a special prayer request for God, write it here:

_____

_____

_____

_____

_____

_____

When Amanda confronted her husband about her discovery, her husband confessed to having multiple affairs. Despite the terrible news, she continued to pray. Subsequently, God provided support and comfort in the way of friends, an infidelity support group, and a husband who was repentant and willing to go to therapy.

In a situation where the discovery is a process and not an immediate event, you may maneuver through a constellation of emotional experiences. You may experience angst, increased suspicion, lack of trust, and hyper-vigilance in monitoring your relationship. Some women choose to ignore warning signs and do not communicate their concerns for fear of a perceived negative outcome, i.e., the dissolution of the marriage. I believe it is important to respect your beliefs and values and to confront your spouse's behaviors in order to be consistent with your values. Even if he chooses to continue his sexual indiscretions, you will know that you practiced assertive behavior and symbolically stood up for the integrity of your value system. Whether you confront unhealthy sexual behaviors or expose lies or duplicitous acts sequentially as you learn of them, or wait until you have a bulk of definitive evidence, is your choice. Lack of confrontation of the affair behaviors rarely leads to cessation of them. Occasionally, the offending spouse's guilt or shame, a major life event, a therapeutic experience (therapy or treatment), or a religious conversion can lead to discontinuation of affair behaviors. However, most individuals have to be confronted or be caught, and must hit rock bottom and experience multiple losses before a sincere behavioral change transpires.

After speaking to several members attending an infidelity support group regarding displays of anger prior to discovery of an affair, it was noted that outbursts of anger and cruel comments are frequently demonstrated by the straying spouse. Rob Bell (2007) in his book, *Sex God: Exploring the Endless Connections Between Sexuality and Spirituality,* noted that lust is the forerunner to despair and anger. After ruling out traditional mental illness, one theory about displays of anger is that the psychological burden of carrying on a duplicitous life becomes so draining that straying spouses begin lashing out at the one with whom they feel the safest. Another hypothesis is that the straying spouse is pushing the marital partner away with hurtful comments or anger, fearful she will leave anyway if confrontations of his behavior have previously occurred. Moreover, his interpersonal effectiveness may be compromised, for he may not be able to be emotionally intimate with his spouse. His inability to effectively convey his needs or desires can result in unconsciously displacing anger in lieu of using effective communication skills. Other reasons for abuse not necessarily related to infidelity consist of lack of respect for partners, a pattern of mistreatment of others witnessed in their families of origin, a dislike of oneself, or a desire to leave the relationship. Regardless of the reason for the abuse or mistreatment, you deserve to be cherished with love, kindness, and respect. God's plan is for you to be loved. Even if your earthly husband is mistreating you, your heavenly bridegroom loves you exceedingly beyond your wildest imagination. You are a jewel who deserves to be esteemed, revered, and nurtured—the way He intended for you to be treated. **You are His**. God proposed to His bride, the nation of Israel, that "Now if you obey me fully and keep my covenant, then out of all nations you will be my treasured possession" (Exodus 19:5 NIV). God described His wife as "treasured." Keeping the sacred covenant meant there was no room for outside lovers and God lamented about His broken heart (Bell, 2007). Israel had become quite adulterous, yet God always continued gestures of love, kindness, and kept His promise. scripture says:

- Husbands, love your wives, just as Christ loved the church and gave himself up for her to make her holy. Ephesians 5:25 (NIV)
- Husbands, in the same way be considerate as you live with your wives, and treat them with respect as the weaker partner and as heirs with you of the gracious gift of life, so that nothing will hinder your prayers. I Peter 3:7 (NIV)
- A kind man benefits himself, but a cruel man brings trouble on himself. Proverbs 11:17 (NIV)
- A man who lacks judgment derides his neighbor, but a man of understanding holds his tongue. Proverbs 11:12 (NIV)
- Do not let any unwholesome talk come out of your mouths, but only what is helpful for building others up according to their needs, that it may benefit those who listen. Ephesians 4:29 (NIV)
- And the second is like it: "Love your neighbor as yourself." Matthew 22:39 (NIV)

Deflection

Upon talking to many betrayed spouses, I discovered that the straying spouse often deflects and points the finger back at the betrayed spouse after discovery and during recovery. The straying spouse attempts to divert attention away from the confronted, illicit behavior, despite clear and actual evidence, and blames other people or circumstances. One therapist shared the delusional thinking of a straying spouse who said, "Are you going to believe what you saw, or are you going to start listening to me?" This comment was made in a therapy session a few months after his wife found him in bed with another woman. Comments or behaviors like these are defense mechanisms to avoid confrontation and perpetuate dishonesty, and to undermine the rational thinking of the betrayed spouse.

Discovery is a painful and traumatic process, and some therapists even liken it to Post Traumatic Stress Disorder (PTSD). Despite the intense pain, there is a desperate attempt to understand and thus most betrayed spouses desire details of the affair(s) to help fit the pieces of the affair puzzle together. The betrayed spouse feels so helpless, powerless, and out of control; that information, no matter how painful, is important for understanding and healing. The disclosure of information is also necessary for straying spouses to demonstrate total and complete honesty if they desire to become whole again and if reconciliation is to transpire. Reconciliation without total and complete honesty is unlikely. Without honesty the relationship will be troubled or difficult to sustain.

Repetitive lies are used to conceal affair behaviors and protect exposure of the clandestine relationship. At some point the lying becomes too difficult for the straying spouse, because the mind can only remember so much. The inconsistencies become exposed and reality and logic prevail. In other words, the stories become contradictory and the liar gets caught in the web of his own lies. scripture advises, "Truthful lips endure forever, but a lying tongue lasts only a moment" (Proverbs 12:19 NIV).

Case Example

Stephanie, a fifty-three-year-old real estate agent, noted feeling infuriated because her spouse's affair story seemed to change every few days. When she inquired about contingent reconciliation, her spouse was not willing to make any behavioral changes that she requested and she couldn't seem to get a straight story from him. He was not willing to go to treatment, he was not willing to stop frequenting strip clubs, and he was not willing to contact his affair partner to terminate the affair. In fact, he was protective of his affair partner "because she is married with three children." Stephanie concluded that her marriage was no longer a priority for her husband. He preferred self-preservation and protecting his affair partner more than the marriage. He was unwilling to demonstrate the total and complete honesty necessary for healing and reconciliation. The negative and unacceptable responses to her requests, although excruciatingly painful, were very revealing and paved the way for her decision to ultimately leave the marriage.

Multiple Losses

Two days after discovering her husband's infidelity, one betrayed spouse learned her mother was formally diagnosed with a life-threatening medical condition. It was a very frightening and depressing time for her. She was fearful of losing her marriage and mother, and yet she knew she had to keep putting one foot in front of the other, to bravely press on to face life's problems. Turn to your faith for strength to carry on. " . . . Forgetting what is behind and straining toward what is ahead, I press on toward the goal to win the prize for which God has called me heavenward in Christ Jesus" (Philippians 3:13-14 NIV).

We are all aware of the very public story of Elizabeth Edwards, who fought and eventually lost her battle with cancer, while simultaneously dealing with the betrayal of her husband. Many women deal with multiple losses, such as miscarriages and infidelity, infertility and infidelity, or medical conditions of self or child and infidelity at the same time. God does not intend for multiple problems to shatter us, but He desires that we learn from them when they occur. From the lens of faith, God permits suffering and uses our circumstances to shape and teach us. "And we know that in all things God works for the good of those who love him, who have been called according to his purpose" (Romans 8:28 NIV). Although God does not promise us life without suffering, he does promise to be with us and comfort us when we face life's tribulations.

- I have told you these things, so that in me you may have peace. In this world you will have trouble. But take heart! I have overcome the world. John 16:33 (NIV)
- But thou, O LORD, art a shield for me; my glory, and the lifter up of mine head. Psalm 3:3 (KJV)
- He maketh me to lie down in green pastures: he leadeth me beside the still waters. He restoreth my soul: he leadeth me in the paths of righteousness for his name's sake. Psalm 23:2-3 (KJV)

- "When you pass through the waters I will be with you; and when you pass through the rivers they will not sweep over you. When you walk through the fire, you will not be burned; the flames will not set you ablaze." Isaiah 43:2-3 (NIV)
- Praise be to the God and Father of our Lord Jesus Christ, the Father of compassion and the God of all comfort, who comforts us in all our troubles, so that we can comfort those in any trouble with the comfort we ourselves have received from God. For just as the sufferings of Christ flow over into our lives, so also through Christ our comfort overflows. I Corinthians 1:3-5 (NIV)
- "As a mother comforts her child, so will I comfort you; and you will be comforted over Jerusalem." Isaiah 66:13 (NIV)
- This is what I covenanted with you when you came out of Egypt. And my Spirit remains among you. Do not fear. Haggai 2:5 (NIV)

Growth from Pain

We don't always get to choose our circumstances in life. In *The Road Less Traveled*, Dr. M. Scott Peck (1978) began his best-selling book by acknowledging the difficulty of life. Isn't that the truth? However, hardships, struggles, and suffering are the core, pivotal experiences that give us opportunities to grow, to develop character, to learn, to gain insight, and to transform as individuals. Without these opportunities we would become listless, lifeless, self-centered people with no need for one another or for God. Peck (1978) noted that it is the entire dynamic of facing and deliberating life's challenges that gives life its true value and generates opportunities for growth and development. Bell (2007) noted that one indicator of personal and spiritual maturation is that of learning to live amongst pain. Accepting the fundamental truth in life that problems do arise and can be seen as opportunities is the first step to managing your pain. Secondly, recognizing that pain is temporary is a helpful realization. Most importantly, knowing that God will be with you during your troubles is a powerful motivator to keep you pressing forward on your healing journey.

Author and psychiatrist Dr. Viktor Frankl (1959), wrote *Man's Search for Meaning*, a book about being a prisoner in a Nazi concentration camp and his subsequent development of Logotherapy. He shares a lesson in which the prisoners embraced their pain and used it as a learning opportunity; they found joy amidst their pain, and enjoyed sharing nature with one another, despite their horrific and brutal circumstances. Frankl (1959) wrote:

> As the inner life of the prisoner tended to become more intense, he also experienced the beauty of art and nature as never before. Under their influence he sometimes even forgot his own frightful circumstances. If someone had seen our faces on the journey from Auschwitz to a Bavarian camp as we beheld the mountains of Salzburg with their summits glowing in the sunset, through the little barred windows of the prison carriage, he would never have believed that those were the faces of men who had given up all hope of life and liberty. Despite that factor—or maybe because of it—we were carried away by nature's beauty, which we had missed for so long.
>
> In camp, too, a man might draw the attention of a comrade working next to him to a nice view of the setting sun shining throughout the tall trees of the Bavarian woods (as in the famous water color by Dürer), the same woods in which we had built an enormous hidden munitions plant. One evening when we were already resting on the floor of our hut, dead tired, soup bowls in hand, a fellow prisoner rushed in and asked us to run out to the assembly grounds and see the wonderful sunset. Standing outside we saw sinister clouds glowing in the west and the whole sky alive with clouds of ever-changing shapes and colors, from steel blue to blood red. The desolate grey mud huts provided a sharp contrast, while the puddles on the muddy ground reflected the glowing sky. Then, after minutes of moving silence, one prisoner said to another, "How beautiful the world *could* be!" (pp. 50-51)

To Stay or Go?

To stay and reconcile your marriage after an affair or to terminate your relationship and divorce is probably one of the most difficult and agonizing decisions you will ever make. My recommendation is to immediately get into counseling to help you process your myriad feelings and to avoid making a hasty decision. Many decisions to divorce are impulsive, and fortunately, most states have a waiting period between filing and finalization. This allows for the possibility of reconciliation or a clearly thought out decision to leave, versus an emotionally reactive one.

Each individual must make his or her own choice about reconciliation or termination of the marriage. Questions to consider when making your decision are:

- Is there complete and total honesty from the straying spouse?
- Is the straying spouse willing to change behavior to build trust?
- Does the straying spouse demonstrate genuine remorse?
- Does the straying spouse demonstrate repentance, showing true regret and devotion toward amending problematic behaviors?
- Has the straying spouse sincerely apologized? (without a "but, you . . . " attached)
- Is the straying spouse willing to answer all the betrayed spouse's questions?
- Is the betrayed spouse willing to work on forgiving the straying spouse?
- Is the betrayed spouse willing to practice being vulnerable and trusting again?
- Is the betrayed spouse willing to attend an infidelity support group, like Beyond Affairs Network (BAN) or find other sources of support for processing and relinquishing the pain and anger?
- Are both parties willing to go to therapy?
- Are both parties willing to assess vulnerability factors within the marriage?
- How will reconciliation or divorce impact the children?
- How will reconciliation or divorce impact my financial situation?
- How will my mental and physical health be impacted?
- Will I have health insurance for me and my children?
- How will my decision affect my future?
- How will my decision impact others (family, mutual friends, church, etc.)?

- Do I have people who will support my decision? If not, what is my plan to find them? And if trusted, respected people do not support my decision, have I considered why?
- What will my living arrangements be?
- What kind of work will I do?
- Do I have adequate emotional, spiritual, and social support?
- Do I have a church that will support my decision?

Write down the answers to all these questions for your own cost/benefit analysis to help you make an educated decision about whether to stay in your marriage, temporarily separate, or file for divorce. Secondly, seek counsel. Ask and poll several people whom you admire and respect and obtain their opinions. Thirdly, read every book you can about infidelity so you can be armed with information. Knowledge is power. The more educated you are on the subject, the better equipped you are to make the most intelligent, healthy, insightful decision that is best for you. Finally and most importantly, pray about your decision. Prayer can provide guidance, confirmation, and peace. More will be discussed about prayer in Chapter 10.

Discussion Questions

1. How did you discover that your partner was having an affair?
2. What are some of the specific factors that make your affair story unique?
3. What is the single most difficult factor about your affair story in which you are having trouble?
4. Are you contemplating leaving the marriage?

Chapter 7

DISCLOSURE

It is my unswerving opinion that after discovery, the betrayed spouse should not suffer in silence, but should disclose the spouse's affair, discuss it in detail and process thoughts and feelings openly to achieve therapeutic healing. This is analogous to Vaughan's (2003) recommendation to oppose the "code of secrecy" about affairs. Furthermore, Bell (2007) noted that regarding general issues of sexuality, it is best to discuss what you are experiencing, for withholding information or using other defense mechanisms never works. There are four reasons for my concurring opinion that sharing is a must. First, to remain silent suggests a secret. Secrets of negativity promote feelings of shame, anxiety, depression, and inadequacy and prohibit interpersonal intimacy with others. Although exposing secrets can be painful initially, sharing is often followed by relief, as healing is halted until the secret is uncovered.

Second, to remain silent is to enable the straying spouse, especially when addictive behaviors are involved. Only by openly discussing the affair with one another and getting feedback from trusted friends, family, clergy, and professionals can the straying spouse be accountable for his or her actions. Complete and total honesty is necessary for the straying spouse to repent, change behaviors, and rebuild trust. scripture supports confession of sin. "When I kept silent, my bones wasted away through my groaning all day long" (Psalm 32:3 NIV). It would be inconsistent to expect the straying spouse to be open and honest, but require the betrayed spouse to keep quiet. Moreover, if the betrayed spouse can share feelings with others, he or she will be more likely to get support and feedback and thus be able to work more quickly through the grieving process. When we are highly emotional, it is often difficult to discern truth from distortion or lies. So disclosing to trusted others allows them to shine light on where we are confused regarding truth versus distortion. When we can clearly see the truth, though it may hurt, we are free as opposed to bound and confined.

Similarly, straying spouses must disclose the affair(s) so they can demonstrate total honesty for confession and repentance. Confessing and repenting shows renewed behaviors of trust and change and begins regenerating the faith and confidence in the marriage.

After discovery of an affair, continued secrets undermine the integrity of the marriage and suggest hiding *more* things and insinuate unchanged behavior. When a clandestine affair is exposed, couples have to start the repair process at square one. Once the discovery process is initiated, it is best for total disclosure to take place so there are no future surprises, otherwise the lies of omission create setbacks for a couple's progression toward reconciliation. In other words, each new secret that is exposed after the original secret places the couple back at square one.

It is best for the straying spouse, despite instincts to disclose minimal details, to use the strategy of total disclosure to avoid delays in healing and reconciliation. The straying spouse has shared something personal and private, the sacred marriage bed, with another and it now no longer retains its privacy and specialness. The straying spouse has broken faith and trust in the marriage and "disclosed" the sacredness of sex to another. The affair, too, must be addressed openly, as opposed to being veiled or protected. Honesty and trust help remove the veil of secrecy and are the personal incubators for developing more intimacy.

Third, there is no research that suggests bottling up pain and omitting discussion about trauma is therapeutic. Therapists in general support honesty and transparency. Being transparent is necessary for growth and development to take place. Recall, we are dealing with a trauma when we are addressing disclosure of infidelity.

Fourth, it is important for a betrayed spouse to speak because he or she may be unknowingly sharing his/her story with someone who may need to hear it or know it at a later time. With infidelity frequencies rising, sharing problems with others is a way to connect with them, role model and pray for others, and to have prayers extended to you. You never know when someone may approach you eight months later with a similar story of infidelity and open up to you because you first shared your pain with them. In other words, pay it forward and give to others a blessing of help and comfort arising from your own suffering and difficulty. "Praise be to the God and Father of our Lord Jesus Christ, the Father of compassion and the God of all comfort, who comforts us in all our troubles, so that we can comfort those in any trouble with the comfort we ourselves have received from God (II Corinthians 1:3-4 NIV). Bell (2007) noted that some of the most reassuring and therapeutic words in the world are "me too." Simply sharing your infidelity pain with another human being may reveal that you are not alone in this crisis. This is why support groups can be so healing. See Chapter 10 on Healing and Nurturing Yourself After Infidelity about the importance of support groups.

In summary, there are a handful of good reasons to share infidelity with others:

- Secrets are unhealthy.
- Secrets are enabling.
- Transparency is therapeutic.
- Sharing promotes closeness with others, and offers role-modeling and prayer opportunities.

To Whom to Disclose?

The first person to disclose to is God. " . . . First seek the counsel of the LORD" (I Kings 22:5 NIV). Always take your troubles, prayers, and concerns to Him first, then seek out earthly counsel. Individuals to use for disclosure are healthy friends and family members, clergy, and mental health professionals. You can assess whether someone will be helpful in supporting you based on your previous and current relationship with them. For example, if your mother is an unhealthy alcoholic with poor boundaries who frequently makes critical statements toward you, she may not be a good choice to disclose personal information to because you may not get the support that you need and deserve. Friends who are supportive, loyal, unconditionally loving, and wise (as opposed to reactive individuals, even if acting out of loyalty to you) are good choices to confide in and to get good, healthy advice. Clergy and counselors are trained to help in crisis marital situations.

One woman recalled sobbing while driving down the highway, grieving that her husband had had his affairs, feeling lost, and not knowing what to do. She felt overwhelmed by pain and out of desperation did a U-turn and drove to the church. She walked in crying, said she was in crisis, and asked to speak to a minister. One of the ministers sat with her for an hour and listened to her story. He was kind and compassionate. They didn't solve any problems from the discussion, for the situation was not changing, but she felt better having shared her feelings. It is amazing what a listening ear can do for one's pain. This is an important example why it is so cathartic to have the freedom to tell your story and share your feelings.

Children: To Tell or Not to Tell?

There is not an universal answer whether or not to disclose the affair to children who are in the family system. Dr. Don-David Lusterman (1998), author of *Infidelity: A Survival Guide*, metaphorically describes infidelity as a speedboat that churns the waters of the family system, leaving children to face the upheaval from their parent's affair. Said in another way, children repeatedly experience the collateral damage of an affair, often for many years or even decades.

Many factors need to be taken into consideration when deciding whether to disclose a parent's affair to children. First, the most important consideration is to protect the children when possible and *always consider their needs*. Children's needs must be placed above your own need to be validated or vindicated. Furthermore, avoid telling children simply to "get them to side with you" or for your own emotional support or comfort. Second, the age, maturity, personality characteristics, and mental health of the children need to be evaluated to determine if it is beneficial to disclose the affair. Third, if discovery or disclosure occurs by happenstance or without choice, be truthful, consistent, and answer questions honestly, accurately, and age appropriately. The following are some case examples for study:

- Bill and Natalie, who reconciled post affair, decided not to disclose the affair to their children because their three children were under age four when the affair occurred.
- James and Laura decided to tell their daughter, who was eighteen years old, but did not disclose the affair to the two younger children, aged twelve and nine, because of their immaturity.
- Jana revealed the affair to both of her children, aged thirteen and six, because her husband left her and married his mistress. Her husband began living with the mistress before the divorce was final, so the children were exposed to the situation. Jana

gave consistent information to both children, although she gave age appropriate answers because of their differences in age and insight.

- Tom and Jen reconciled post affair; they had two teenage boys aged fifteen and sixteen. One son struggled with depression and self-mutilation. Tom and Jen decided that they would not disclose the affair because they were concerned that their son's mental health condition would deteriorate. Since the boys' ages were so close together, they were not comfortable telling only one son about the affair. They thought that revealing the affair would put pressure on one to keep a secret from the other. They opted not to tell either son.

- Robert and Amy stayed together after Amy's affair, and they decided not to disclose the affair currently to their six- and nine-year-old girls. With infidelity being a family pattern, it is their desire to tell the children about the affair when they are older in an attempt to educate them about affair-prevention.

- Payton, after learning of her husband's philandering and serial affairs, filed for divorce. She chose not to disclose the infidelity to her eleven-year-old daughter. Payton reported she wanted her daughter to have a positive view of her father, and the marital issues were "adult information that children do not need to worry about."

Because affairs are irrational behaviors, it rarely occurs to the straying spouse that these behaviors may have a great impact on others. Consequences can be far-reaching, impacting many individuals: spouses, children, extended family, friends, neighbors, church members, professional coworkers, and clients. In other words, it seldom strikes a straying spouse when having affairs that the behaviors can have such extensive ripple effects on other people.

Betrayed spouses have an opportunity to serve others and ultimately glorify God with how they respond to affairs. You have a choice and an opportunity to be a role model of grace and integrity while handling difficult circumstances when you have been wronged. You can use this gift of suffering to teach people to use pain as a tool for growth. "Each one should use whatever gift he has received to serve others, faithfully administering God's grace in its various forms" (I Peter 4:10).

There will be times when you fall short of grace, eagerly desiring pity and self-righteous vindication for being wronged. Although natural and human, but not virtuous, this reveals one's own need for growth. Other times, you may respond like a champ, only by the power of the Holy Spirit, not of your own merit. The growth-provoking effects of pain on the innocent party help keep betrayed spouses from becoming martyrs. This growth-building process allows you to see the "less than grace-filled" traits that emerge from within. For a visual image, it is much like a teacup that gets jostled. We are each responsible for what is in our own teacup, i.e., our personal reactions even when jostled, provoked, or mistreated. Whatever spills out is not the "jostler's" fault, for what spills out is what was already in the cup.

What one betrayed spouse came to value most from her experience from the pain of infidelity is her subsequent closer, deeper, more intimate relationship with God. She came to experience a longing; a craving, an intense hunger to know more about God and His scriptures. This kind of yearning may only be possible through hardship. God will be your constant companion throughout the sorrow. You may want to talk to Him with more fervent prayers during this time of pain and suffering. He will be forever faithful, like a rock, a fortress, never forsaking you. Always present, always hearing and seeing, and never-changing is our God. Characteristics or names of our steadfast God found in scripture that give comfort and strength:

- She gave this name to the LORD who spoke to her: "You are the God who sees me," for she said, "I have now seen the One who sees me." Genesis 16:13 (NIV)
- LORD, my strength and my fortress, and my refuge in the day of affliction. Jeremiah 16:19 (KJV)
- There is none holy as the LORD: for there is none besides thee: neither is there any rock like our God. I Samuel 2:2 (KJV)
- I the LORD do not change . . . Malachi 3:6 (NIV)
- . . . I will never leave you nor forsake you. Joshua 1:5 (NIV)

When you disclose your story to some, you may hear some gems of wisdom. Your dear friends and family will give you warm words of advice. Support group members will wish you well after each meeting and you will pick up on special "nuggets" of growth and healing. One woman reported one of the best pieces of advice is to understand that healing from infidelity is a grieving process. Furthermore, it is important to remember that grief comes in spurts. This simple reminder can liberate you to give yourself permission to allow your grief to come naturally. Permit your grief to come when it needs to, and how it needs to—sporadically, in spurts, or however it idiosyncratically presents itself. There may be days where the betrayed spouse is feeling strong and then, all of a sudden, she is grieved. Remember that God is with you during every moment of your grief.

- But you, O God, do see trouble and grief; you consider it to take it in hand. Psalm 10:14 (NIV)
- Blessed are those who mourn, for they will be comforted. Matthew 5:4 (NIV)
- I tell you the truth, you will weep and mourn while the world rejoices. You will grieve, but your grief will turn to joy. John 16:20 (NIV)
- This poor man cried, and the LORD heard him, and saved him out of all his troubles. Psalm 34:6 (KJV)
- Blessed be God, even the Father of our Lord Jesus Christ, the Father of mercies, and the God of all comfort. II Corinthians 1:3 (KJV)

How Friends and Family can Help

Friends and family can help betrayed spouses in several ways. First, they can surround them with unconditional support and love without condemnation. Second, they will never assume the betrayed spouse "caused" the affair. Third, they can encourage and allow the betrayed spouse to express anger, an often invalidated emotion in our society, especially for women. Allowing them to process their anger promotes their healing journey and diffuses the double standard among anger expression between the sexes.

Caveats for Disclosure of Infidelity

In the midst of disorientation, sense of injustice and betrayal, and emotional rawness, it is an understatement to say that discernment regarding disclosure of an affair is difficult. One betrayed spouse later joked about revealing her affair to the grocery store clerk. The clerk asked, "How are you today?" and she unloaded on him. At times, you want to tell anyone who will listen. Although sharing your pain is normal, here are some guidelines to help aid you in determining how much to share and with whom.

The key to discerning disclosure is determining a healthy mental poise about revealing your pain to others without personal disclosure that will greatly add to the already present damage. In other words, we want to achieve a balance between too much disclosure (over-exposure) and pretense and hiding (not enough disclosure). A good rule of thumb is to evaluate each situation on a case-by-case basis.

| **Secrecy** | **Balance** | **Over-Disclosure** |
| **Damage to Self** | | **Damage to Self/Others** |

After the discovery of an affair, the future of the relationship is unknown. For this reason, it is wise to consider how sharing the affair with others may impact them, you, and your family system, if reconciliation is a possibility. For example, if an affair is disclosed to family members of the betrayed spouse, will the family members later accept reconciliation of the marriage and forgive the straying spouse and treat him respectfully? Another thing to consider is whether or not to disclose the affair to the straying spouse's employer if the affair happened in the workplace. One betrayed spouse's aunt called the straying spouse's employer and alerted the boss of his affair with a subordinate. He ended up losing his job, and this later impacted the family system because he was unable to pay child support when the couple divorced. Although the relative's anger was valid and she was attempting to protect the betrayed spouse, the disclosure had damaging financial effects on the family.

It is important to stay connected to your convictions, and remain discerning in regard to how you talk about affairs to others. Not sharing at all destroys with its secrecy, but over-disclosure can be damaging to self, to others, and to the relationship, especially if reconciliation is a possibility. Deciding to whom to disclose can be a journey of self-examination and course correction. To achieve "healing with humility," it is helpful for betrayed spouses to get to a place of understanding their intentions for disclosure, rather than focusing on what the straying spouse did. Make sure your disclosure is not motivated by revenge or other wrong motives. Avoid "spreading the poison," which may later leave you feeling regretful or could cause additional negative repercussions. For example, one betrayed spouse chose to share her story with neighbors. After she and her husband reconciled, the straying husband felt awkward at neighborhood functions and it impacted their social life. Neighbors had a hard time accepting the reconciled marriage because of their knowledge of his previous affair.

Guidelines for Disclosure with Discernment

- Assess each situation on a case-by-case basis.
- Stay connected to your convictions.
- Carefully evaluate those to whom you plan to disclose.
- Aim for a healthy balance between secrecy and over-disclosure.
- Ask yourself, *"How will the future be affected if this person knows about the affair?"*

Discussion Questions

1. To whom did you decide to reveal the affair?
2. To whom did you decide to conceal the affair?
3. What impact does the future have on deciding to whom to reveal?

CHAPTER 8

THE AFFAIR PARTNER

Who is she? Who is this woman(en)who has come into your marriage unprecedented, unannounced, and with whom your husband has become intimately involved? Who is this woman who has violated what you held so sacredly in your covenant relationship? Who is this woman with whom your husband would go to extraordinary lengths to lie and deceive you when you thought he was working late, having a beer with the guys, or even at a prayer meeting at church? Who is this other woman with whom your husband would have sex while you were battling cancer, pregnant with twins, recently miscarried, or struggling with infertility?

Basically, she could be *any* woman. She could be me or you. None of us is exempt from the vulnerabilities of sexual sin, and it behooves us to gain wisdom and learn ways to protect and safeguard ourselves from the temptations and traps of sexual misconduct. What may begin as innocent flirting in a misdemeanor style can lead to greater, felonious transgressions of adulterous behavior.

According to Carder (1992), one common characteristic that affair partners may share when sexual addictions are present is that they may be financially inferior to the straying spouse. He noted this maintains the straying spouse's position of power, objectifies the affair partner, and perpetuates the addiction.

This other woman, the affair partner, may initially pursue the straying spouse or the straying spouse may instigate the relationship with the other woman. Each is responsible for participating in the illicit relationship. It is really inconsequential who initiated the affair, because the pain for the betrayed spouse is connected with the affair itself.

The other woman may generally be a "play-by-the-rules" person, or a well-mannered individual who is simply making unhealthy choices by becoming involved with an unavailable, married partner. Some are religious individuals who have fallen astray from their walk with God and who make one-time mistakes, such as a fling. Some participate in ongoing affairs. Others continually seek out married men to avoid intimacy and long-term commitments. Still others are cold and callous and see the wives of men as merely competition, unconcerned about the destruction of the family system. Some affair partners are repentant and feel guilt and empathy, some do not. In other words, each "other woman" can be very different. This "other woman," who is often feared and hated, can provide you with an unforeseen blessing. The gift of suffering permits you to transform raw hurt and pain to hope, healing, and forgiveness transcended over time, although it will likely take a while to view the affair partner through this lens.

Case Example

Gracelyn, a thirty-five-year-old dance instructor, sought therapy with me after her relationship with a married man was discovered by his wife and subsequently terminated. We determined through therapy that she had a repetitive pattern of seeking out unavailable men that commonly ended up with destructive outcomes that mimicked the detachment and unavailability of her emotionally distant father. She typically displayed patterns of emotional guardedness and self-protection, although she had fallen in love with her lover. Despite his unavailability, she was severely wounded when the relationship ended. She did feel sorry for the betrayed spouse, but never enough to consider terminating the affair. She fantasized about resuming the relationship with her lover if he were to extend the invitation. She never set out to purposely hurt the betrayed spouse, but she was unable to have adequate empathy for her because she was consumed by her own pain.

Are Affairs Accidental or Purposeful?

Affairs are, for the most part, unplanned. Most straying spouses don't wake up one day and intend and contrive to "hurt their spouse" by having an affair. Most affairs develop gradually over time, much like a traditional relationship. Affairs often begin in a neutral place, like the coffee break room at the office, and progressively develop into an affair. Few happen overnight or on purpose. Nonetheless, there are a few exceptions. The first is the retaliatory or "revenge affair" that some engage in to pay back a spouse for the hurt caused by a primary affair. These affairs are futile and fruitless. Revenge affairs do nothing but cause more hurt and pain and undermine the integrity of the relationship which makes reconciliation all the more challenging. During revenge affairs, affair partners may be selected at random on a "first come, first serve" basis—whoever is available and willing so the revenge can take place quickly. On the other hand, the affair partner may be calculatingly handpicked to exact deep pain: an ex-lover, a visible neighbor, or a coworker, to inflict vivid reminders on the spouse who had the original affair.

A second possible exception to the rule that affairs are not premeditated is the "exit affair," to be explored more in detail later in this chapter. The motivation for exit affairs can be, at times, partly unconscious, most people having no idea the extent of the enormous amount of pain they are causing. Exit affairs are not always as planned or strategic as revenge affairs, although they can be.

Pittman (1989) noted that it is *not* a compliment to be selected as an affair partner. Because relationships borne out of affairs rarely turn into healthy marriages, selection of affair partners is usually based on some idiosyncratic, unhealthy reason(s). He further noted that the selection of affair partners is more likely to be chosen based on their differences from the spouse, rather than them being in some way superior to the spouse, as the betrayed spouse often assumes and fears.

Pittman (1989) noted, "I certainly have not found a pattern of affair partners being better-looking than marriage partners, or nicer, or more accomplished . . . To my subjective eye, affairees have not tended to be a startlingly good-looking group" (p.42-43).

One woman reported feeling comforted when she learned at a BAN meeting that affair partners are not particularly more attractive. This knowledge gave her and other group members reassurance and consolation. It was comforting to realize that they were not out-beautified by the affair competition, as was evident for those betrayed spouses who actually saw the affair partner in person. There is something instinctual about women's longing to be seen as beautiful and to be desired by their husbands. Some betrayed spouses saw the affair partner by choice, others by happenstance, but they were often surprised to learn she was less attractive than envisioned. Many betrayed spouses often distortedly imagine the affair partner to be a gorgeous supermodel, when this is typically not the case.

Let's explore several possible rationales and case examples to aid in understanding other motivations for affair partner selection: compensation for individual differences, exit affairs, supplementation to the marriage, and reconnection with former lovers. One, previously mentioned, is that the straying spouse is choosing the affair partner to compensate for differences between the individuals, not necessarily inferiority of the spouse.

Exit Affairs

As stated, the straying spouse may be choosing an affair partner in order to leave the relationship, commonly known as an exit affair. Selection of exit affair partners is often random and occurs by happenstance—whoever is available and shows the straying spouse attention at the time.

Case Examples

Stephen, a young newlywed married for two years, reported to me that he was so unhappy in his marriage that he just chose the first woman who would pay attention to him and go to bed with him because he knew his wife would not leave him unless he gave her a "biblical reason." As soon as his divorce was final, he ditched his affair partner, who felt used and devastated. She was so distraught that she attempted suicide and was admitted to the local psychiatric hospital.

Monty, on the other hand, a twenty-eight-year-old graduate student of physics, desired a divorce from his overbearing wife, but was so codependent that he did not want to be alone after the divorce. He chose an exit affair, but wanted to secure his next relationship and have a girlfriend "waiting in the wings." Monty became involved in a relationship for several months and then mustered up the courage and broke the news to his wife. She was enraged and, surprisingly to Monty, forgave him and refused to file for divorce. So, he eventually decided to file. Last I heard, he was living with his affair partner. Pittman(1989) described this type of affair relationship as a "rescuing relationship" characterized by instant gratification and impulsivity.

Supplementation

Some affair partners are chosen to "supplement" the marriage. Pittman (1989) noted that "more often people are not seeking an alternative to their marriage, but a supplement to it" (p. 43). The straying spouse is choosing the affair partner to meet needs that the spouse is allegedly or seemingly not meeting at home, whether those needs be sexual or a need for friendship, recreation, communication, or romance. However, the illicit relationship often turns sexual, violating the vows of marital commitment. A common colloquialism states, "They want their cake and to eat it, too." Those lured by lust must learn to shun and circumvent entitlement through self-awareness and accountability. Individuals susceptible to affairs must develop wholesome and nonthreatening ways of supplementing their marriages without violating their faithfulness and honesty to their spouses. Examples of healthy supplementation would be attending a Bible study, book club, participating in a sports team, engaging in a hobby or craft, or exercising. Activities with others of the opposite sex require accountability, honesty, self-discipline, and self-disclosure to one's spouse, if marriages are to remain protected from affairs.

Reconnection with a Former Lover

Affair partners may be selected because they have a former connection from one's past romantic history, particularly from an unresolved relationship. With the invention of the Internet, Facebook, cellular phones, and more frequent business travel for many, it is quite economically and technologically simple to connect with people from one's past despite geographic restrictions. Some individuals have lost loves and pine over former lovers. They frequently look them up online or on Facebook to check their status, which is a dangerous temptation. Former relationships that did not work for various and significant reasons should stay former and closed. One way to cherish your current spouse is to make him or her your one-and-only. Communication with a former lover should rarely exist. One appropriate exception would be for the purpose of co-parenting shared children following termination of a relationship.

Areas for Further Research

It came to my attention while observing infidelity in my practice that a good number of straying spouses selected affair partners of a different race. I found scarce research on this topic, but found this characteristic to be nonetheless interesting. It would be a good dissertation topic for an eager doctoral student. Interracial relationships are becoming more common in our society, although they are not yet the norm. I noticed that a car commercial paired an interracial couple together in a Christmas ad for the first time last year.

Most betrayed spouses considered the racial difference of the affair partner to be an additional obstacle in healing. One Caucasian patient in my practice was highly disturbed that her husband had had an affair with an African-American woman. As a result, she came to despise all African-American women. Every time she encountered one, she was painfully reminded of the affair. Although this was irrational and distorted thinking, the fact that her husband chose an affair partner outside of his race was an additional issue for her to overcome.

Interestingly, had her husband chosen a Caucasian woman with whom to have an affair, she probably wouldn't have begun to despise all Caucasian women. She wouldn't have necessarily been reminded of the affair each time she saw another Caucasian woman, simply because of the larger number of them with whom she came into contact. Perhaps my patient had less frequent dealings with women from minority groups. They seemed to stand out and my patient began to over-generalize and associate them all as one racial unit that could not be trusted. All in all, the difference in race of an affair partner adds another layer of pain for the betrayed spouse to sort through, likely due to the sharp contrast between them or prejudicial beliefs.

Discussion Questions

1. Did you know your spouse's affair partner?
2. Have you decided whether or not to contact the affair partner?
3. How did the identity of the affair partner impact your healing journey?

CHAPTER 9

VULNERABILITY FACTORS

Vulnerability factors are issues that increase a relationship's fragility and susceptibility to breaches of trust. Vulnerability factors are present in all marriages and are *never* excuses for affairs. Vulnerability factors can be temporary, situational, chronic, or permanent, depending on circumstances or the dynamics of personalities or maturity of the partners. Vulnerability factors may impact one or both individuals emotionally in the marriage, and, subsequently may lead to temptation for one or both members of the relationship. Furthermore, vulnerability factors may emerge gradually over time, may erupt spontaneously and surprisingly, or may be inherent from the inception of the relationship.

Subotnik and Harris (2005) suggested the equivalent of relationship vulnerability is "transitional anxiety." They stated that anxiety concerning life's transitional issues or stages is often a precursor for affairs. For example, it could be an actual event that occurs, such as the loss of a child, or an event that does not happen, such as the inability to get pregnant. Subotnik and Harris (2005) cited several examples of transitional anxiety that are worthy of mentioning (pp. 35-49):

- Losses (death, separation, or divorce)
- Gains (births, marriages, promotions)
- Midlife crisis
- Teenagers, parenting difficulties
- Caring for aging parents
- Children leaving for college
- Difficulty accepting the aging process
- Sexual impotence
- Unfulfilled expectations
- Unrealistic ideas about love and marriage

- Need for attention
- Boredom
- Unavailable spouse (geographically, or due to a mental or physical condition, or travel, or military service)
- Lack of sexual desire (in one or both parties)
- "Poor risk partner" (e.g., narcissistic tendencies)

It is important to properly assess and identify vulnerability factors in your marriage. A common colloquialism is, "A good part of the solution is a well-defined problem." This gives you a leg up on preventing affairs in the future. Second, it is imperative to openly discuss vulnerability factors as soon as they arise. Waiting or delaying discussion is dangerous, especially if affairs at any level have previously occurred. Avoidance of communication hinders intimacy and reduces the health of the relationship. Set aside time each week to discuss vulnerability issues to establish healthy communication routines and build accountability. Write the issues down on paper.

Third, develop strategies to minimize their impact when possible. Put the strategies or goals on the same piece of paper as the vulnerability factors. Put the goals in a visible place, perhaps on your refrigerator door or your bathroom mirror, so you can monitor your relationship progress daily. Fourth, accept or adapt to vulnerability issues that are unchangeable. Some vulnerability issues are unalterable and cause permanent limitations to the relationship. Discuss how these issues impact your marriage and how you will make accommodations for them. Again, write them down on paper, along with the adaptations you have accepted.

Identification of vulnerability factors helps us understand some of the reasons people choose to have affairs. I interviewed Brian Bercht, co-author of *My Husband's Affair Became the Best Thing That Ever Happened to Me*, who has created a vulnerability scale instrument (personal communication December 1, 2010). He stated that this 300-question instrument helps to "answer the whys" of affairs. He reported he designed the instrument as a project to help explore and understand "why I did what I did." He developed the vulnerability scale as he and his wife, Anne Bercht, have devoted their lives to helping couples and individuals recover from affairs. The scale is ever changing and Bercht adds new vulnerability factors to it as he learns more about affair behaviors through his work.

Bercht noted that most straying spouses did not score less than seventy-five on his instrument. Most straying spouses scored in the range of 150 to 180. Furthermore, he noted that most straying spouses he has worked with were experiencing depression at the time of the affair. This instrument is unique in its scope and practical usefulness. It is an excellent tool to help couples identify the trouble areas within themselves and within their marriage that could lead to fragility of the relationship and susceptibility to extramarital affairs. In other words, it is a useful measure to help couples safeguard their marriages from future affairs.

Case Example

Clark and Leah came to couples therapy six months after each had participated in an extramarital affair. Each affair had occurred independently, meaning neither was retaliatory. Upon exploration in therapy, we uncovered the following ten vulnerability issues:

1. Job loss for Clark
2. Temporary financial strain during period of unemployment
3. Death of Leah's grandmother
4. Birth of twin boys
5. Sexual dysfunction for Clark
6. Leah's mother having had an affair
7. Leah's low self-esteem and need for admiration from men
8. Clark's penchant for pornography and strip clubs
9. Son's medical condition (asthma)
10. Hesitancy for both in discussing the affairs because of shame

Let's assess each one of their vulnerability factors and analyze them in terms of their short or long-term potential. In other words, let's look to see if the vulnerability factors are temporary, chronic, or permanent. This can help a couple understand the dynamics that affect the integrity of the marriage and aid them in constructing a plan to strengthen and fortify the relationship with an overall goal of fidelity.

The first vulnerability factor identified for this couple was Clark's job loss. Being laid off from one's employer can be a big blow. Not only was it a surprise, but it came six months after the babies were born. Clark also prided his ego on his ability to provide for his family.

What Happens After Shattered?

He saw his work as his identity. When he was unable to secure a new job immediately, he felt inadequate and humiliated. This led him to seek validation outside the marriage. The job layoff vulnerability factor can be seen as a temporary and short-term vulnerability factor, because Clark eventually procured employment. The job loss impacted the family financially, which led to vulnerability factor number two.

Temporary financial strain was a vulnerability factor for both Clark and Leah. Because unemployment benefits only covered a portion of regular bills, they began to dip into their small savings to make ends meet. Soon the savings were gone and they resorted to using credit cards. This sent Clark's anxiety through the roof. He began to be more vocal about reducing their spending and this irritated Leah. Leah did not change her spending habits—in fact, she began to spend recklessly. They had numerous fights about finances. Leah began reaching out to her affair partner to help meet her financial needs. This particular vulnerability factor is temporary, because financial situations are variable. Although getting out of debt can take a long time, if two people are committed to a budget, their financial situation can be changeable. Once Clark became re-employed and Leah recognized her overspending habits, they were able to work out a monthly budget to which they both agreed.

The third vulnerability factor noted was the death of Leah's grandmother. Although a death itself is always permanent, the grief and loss will change with time. Leah had essentially been raised by her grandmother after her mother left her and her sister because of her addiction. Leah's father had died in a work related accident a few years before. The death of a loved one can render one more fragile, depressed, and vulnerable, especially at the time of the death or during the grief process. Leah's grandmother played a central role in her life by being her primary caregiver when her parents were unavailable. It is important to assess how a death impacts the individual and the marriage and develop techniques to adapt to the loss. The impact on the marriage also depends on the relationship of the deceased. For example, the death of a child will have a profound and longer lasting impact on the marriage than, say, a distant relative.

It is also important to assess if the individual has experienced multiple losses in life or during a short period of time preceding the infidelity. Sometimes, current losses can trigger the grief of previous losses during childhood or earlier times in life, thus complicating and intensifying the present pain.

The birth of twins was a new transition and brought additional vulnerability for both Clark and Leah. Clark felt displaced by the twins getting all of the family's attention, and Leah felt overwhelmed with her new role as a mother. She felt as if she was being a single parent, not receiving enough help from Clark. Many times, she was feeding both babies, one in each arm, while Clark was snoozing in the bedroom. This infuriated Leah. Clark, because of his own feelings of inadequacy, did not know how to help and therefore "checked out."

The birth of children can be a challenging time for new parents. Although the baby phase is temporary, it is followed by different developmental phases in childhood. Perhaps the baby phase is one of the most life-altering phases for new parents because they are now responsible for the complete care of a tiny human being and their lifestyle is dramatically different from before. The marital relationship is radically changed, with new responsibilities being added and flexibility being taken away. The birth of children is considered to be a long-term vulnerability factor, if not never-ending.

An additional vulnerability factor was Clark's sexual dysfunction. Although many men experience sexual dysfunction, (i.e., Erectile Dysfunction (ED), Premature ejaculation (PME), or lack of orgasm), Clark initially refused to be evaluated and instead blamed Leah for his troubles. He insisted it was not his problem since his sexual performance was not impacted when he viewed pornography or engaged sexually with his affair partner, who was a stripper. Clark's insistence that his dysfunction was Leah's fault led Leah to begin to question her attractiveness. She began to suffer feelings of inadequacy and found the attention of other men validating.

Sexual dysfunction, when properly treated by a physician or a sex therapist, can be a temporary condition. This can be a temporary vulnerability factor as long as an individual is willing to seek treatment, assuming the individual is not diagnosed with a medical condition that prohibits sexual activity. If sexual intercourse is impossible because of a general medical condition, then couples need to develop a plan to engage in alternative forms of affection to maintain high levels of emotional intimacy. Certain medications can cause sexual side effects or sexual dysfunction so it is important to see your healthcare professional for regular evaluations.

Sexual dysfunction can be caused by emotional or psychological factors, specifically a "self-centered" approach to sex, rather than an "other-centered" approach to sex. Some individuals develop sexual dysfunction because of unrealistic expectations of marital sex, or they may have a distorted perception of sacred marital sex. These individuals tend to hyper-focus on always having their physical needs met, be preoccupied with sexual technique, or get easily bored with the routine of marital sex. These individuals are particularly susceptible to seeking out novelty or risk, often in search of sexual "fireworks" from an affair. Eventually, novelty wears off, even with the affair partner, and the sexual dysfunction returns.

Another vulnerability factor was the family history of affair behavior. Leah's mother had had affairs with men in her hometown prior to Leah's parents' divorce and her dad's subsequent death. A common saying is "An apple doesn't fall far from the tree." As previously mentioned, individuals who witnessed their primary caregivers having affairs are more likely to participate in affairs themselves, perhaps because they view the habits as normal (Pittman, 1989). Furthermore, individuals may unconsciously choose unreliable spouses, those who are more prone to have affairs, if affairs were witnessed in their family of origin.

If one of your parents has had an affair, this is a type of permanent vulnerability factor, because the past cannot be changed (although your response to the past can be changed). Do not fault yourself for your family history, but be wise and see it as a useful warning sign. It does not mean you or your partner *will* have an affair, it just signifies an elevated risk factor. Some people have vehement reactions against their parent's affair, making declarations like, *"I will never do to my family what my Dad did to my Mom!"* Nonetheless, pay attention to this vulnerability factor, for to overlook it would be negligent. Just like we can benefit from genetic testing to determine if we may be susceptible to certain diseases, learning about a family history of affairs gives us some powerful information for affair-prevention.

The next vulnerability factor that was assessed was Leah's low self-esteem and need for validation from men. I defined this to be a chronic vulnerability factor. Since Leah was abandoned by her parents, had not had a stable male figure in her life since the death of her father, and witnessed her mother's string of unhealthy relationships with men, she had low self-esteem and sought sexual validation through men outside the marriage. Seeking validation outside the marriage was modeled as a "coping" strategy by her mother.

Clark's addiction to pornography and strip clubs was also a vulnerability factor in the marriage. Clark began to use pornography and sexually-oriented businesses to boost his ego and get sexual release when he was unable to perform sexually with his wife. I also defined this vulnerability factor to be a chronic problem, because he used pornography and strip clubs to maladaptively fight a long history of feeling unworthy. The difference between chronic and permanent vulnerability factors is that chronic problems can be changed with a treatment plan and a patient's desire to change. Although some chronic problems may be long-term in their duration, few vulnerability factors are permanent. This is said to give you hope and encouragement that personal issues and relationships can be helped and healed. "So do not fear, for I am with you; do not be dismayed, for I am your God" (Isaiah 41:10 NIV).

Another vulnerability factor defined for Clark and Leah was the asthma diagnosis given to one of their sons. This medical condition proved to be stressful for them because it included several misdiagnoses, multiple doctor visits and trips to the ER, and scary breathing treatments. Although the pediatrician thinks that their son will eventually grow out of asthma, for them it is a real and current vulnerability factor. They need to place it on the list for as long as it is an issue.

A final vulnerability issue discovered in therapy was the couple's hesitancy to discuss their respective affairs. Lack of total disclosure and honesty created tension and contributed to an obstacle in rebuilding trust after the infidelities. This vulnerability factor was defined as short-term as the couple became more skilled and willing to discuss the affair behaviors over time.

Here is an outline of the vulnerability factors for Clark and Leah. They made a chart and defined the type of vulnerability factor and their plans to address each issue. They chose to place their list on their bathroom mirror so they would see it daily, discuss it each morning as they were getting ready for the day, and practice talking more openly about their relationship issues.

<u>Clark and Leah's Plan:</u>

1. **<u>Vulnerability Factor:</u>** Job Loss

   <u>Type</u>: (Short-term)

   - Begin therapy immediately if job loss occurs to process grief, planning, and affair-prevention

   - Maintain accountability group attendance during job search

   - Begin career support group at church

   - Always have resume updated

   - Regularly attend networking lunches

2. **<u>Vulnerability Factor:</u>** Temporary Financial Strain

   <u>Type</u>: (Short-term)

   - Develop a financial budget in which both parties agree

   - Develop an emergency fund for financial crisis situations

   - Agree to curb spending during crisis situations

   - Attend therapy to address the effects of financial stress on each: Clark (anxiety) and Leah (spending)

3. **<u>Vulnerability Factor</u>**: Death of Grandmother

   <u>Type</u>: (Short-term)

   - Join a grief support group

   - Read a bereavement book

   - Visit grandmother's grave

   - Design a scrapbook with pictures of grandmother

   - Talk to sister about feelings of loss and fond memories of grandmother

- Volunteer time at a charitable organization in honor of grandmother

4. **Vulnerability Factor**: Birth of Twin Sons

   Type: (Long-term)

   - Engage in therapy to discuss feelings related to being parents

   - Discuss how becoming parents has changed the marital relationship

   - Schedule date nights twice a month for couples time

   - Schedule time for sexual intimacy

   - Take a parenting class together

   - Read a parenting book together

5. **Vulnerability Factor:** Sexual Dysfunction

   Type: (Short-term)

   - Visit with personal physician to rule out medical problems

   - Consider a medication evaluation (rule out side effects of current medications or consider medications for sexual dysfunction)

   - Eliminate pornography and strip club attendance

   - Join Sex and Love Addicts Anonymous (SLAA) since sexual addiction symptoms are present

   - Participate in individual therapy with a therapist who specializes in sex therapy

   - Read a book on sexual dysfunction

6. **Vulnerability Factor**: Family History of Extramarital Affairs

   Type: (Permanent)

   - Openly discuss family history without secrets or shame

- Make a verbal commitment to renew vows

- Read a book about marriage building

7. **Vulnerability Factor:** Low Self-Esteem and Need for Male Admiration

   Type: (Chronic)

   - Participate in individual therapy to address self-esteem and need for admiration due to family of origin issues

   - Purchase and complete a workbook with exercises to improve self-esteem

   - Obtain an accountability partner to address the need for admiration from men

   - Write down five self-affirmations and recite daily

   - Establish a new hobby to boost self-esteem

   - Nurture social relationships with female friends to reduce the need for male affirmation

8. **Vulnerability Factor:** Pornography and Strip Club Attendance

   Type: (Chronic)

   - Attend individual therapy to process emotional issues

   - Join Sex and Love Addicts Anonymous (SLAA) and obtain a sponsor

   - Join an accountability group at church

   - Obtain an accountability partner at church who is sober and values monogamy

   - Read a book on sexual addiction

   - Agree to have accountability software installed on all home computers and devices

9. **Vulnerability Factor:** Son's Medical Condition: Asthma

    Type: (Chronic)

    - Follow all treatment plans recommended by physician

    - Attend an asthma support group together

    - Read a book on pediatric asthma

    - Take turns giving son breathing treatments

10. **Vulnerability Factor:** Hesitancy to Discuss Affair Behaviors

    Type: (Short-term)

    - Make a commitment to discuss the affairs in therapy and at home

    - Write down questions you have for one another about the affairs

    - Set aside a certain time each week to discuss the relationship

    - Put the vulnerability factor list and goals on the bathroom mirror to reflect the importance of discussing the affairs and the marital relationship

To develop your own goals to identify and combat vulnerability issues, see the Vulnerability Factor Worksheet in Appendix B at the end of the book.

Discussion Questions

1. What vulnerability factors were you able to identify in yourself?
2. What vulnerability factors were you able to identify in your spouse?
3. Do you believe vulnerability factors are excuses for affairs?
4. Do you believe that identifying vulnerability factors can help explain the "whys" of affairs?

Chapter 10

HEALING & NURTURING
YOURSELF AFTER INFIDELITY

This chapter will explore therapeutic activities to address the pain of infidelity and to aid and promote your healing journey. Ideas discussed will be prayer, therapy, medication, exercise, journaling, support group attendance, bibliotherapy, and nurturing activities.

Prayer

People have been praying for thousands of years. Prayer, although unable to be understood scientifically because it is a concept based on faith, has a spiritual, healing quality for us, as we surrender our problems to God. Much larger than us, God is better equipped and able to handle our requests when we are helpless, powerless, or out of control. A patient recently remarked to me that she feels "a sense of peace and relief" when she prays.

The first recorded prayer in the Bible is by Eve in the book of Genesis in the Old Testament. Eve desired to commend the Lord by lifting up a prayer of praise when she acknowledged God for giving her a son. " . . . She said, 'With the help of the LORD I have brought forth a man" (Genesis 4:1 NIV). She named him Cain and then had a second son, Abel. Later in the same chapter, Cain kills his brother Abel out of jealousy. Cain's prayer of petition to God is the second recorded prayer in the Bible as he fears for his life after God curses him with restless wandering and a harvestless crop from the land. He petitions God with a prayer, out of fear that he will be killed during his restless roaming.

> Cain said to the LORD, "My punishment is more than I can bear. Today you are driving me from the land, and I will be hidden from your presence; I will be a restless wanderer on the earth, and whoever finds me will kill me" (Genesis 4:13-14 NIV).

God answers Cain mercifully and protects him by marking him and stating that anyone who murders Cain will suffer compounded revenge. "But the LORD said to him, 'Not so; if anyone kills Cain, he will suffer vengeance seven times over.' The LORD put a mark on Cain so that no one who found him would kill him" (Genesis 4:15 NIV).

Prayer is an important part of healing. It keeps us connected to our Heavenly Father. It reminds us that we do not have to do life alone, that we have a parent watching out for us, taking care of us. We simply have to remember to reach out and ask. Eve and Cain dialogued with God for different reasons, but both stayed attached to Him by maintaining contact with Him, either by praise or through petition. Whether we are joyous or troubled, it is helpful to reach out to God in prayer. Eve was delighted to give honor to God for gifting her with a child. Cain, on the other hand, realized his error and felt the terror of being out of the Lord's presence. He became scared and drew nearer to the Lord out of fear which prompted his desperate prayer. Whether our prayers are to honor God or to initiate personal requests, He delights in each one. " . . . For the LORD will take delight in you . . . " (Isaiah 62:4 NIV). God is so awesome and mighty that he hears every prayer and listens attentively. "I call on you, O God, for you will answer me; give ear to me, and hear my prayer" (Psalm 17:6 NIV). We may not *always* get the answer we are looking for, in the time frame we are looking for, or in the way that we are looking for; but, we can rest assured that our omniscient, omnipotent God knows what we have prayed and that He knows what is best for us.

Prayers of Petition

Prayers of petition, those prayers defined as asking for something for the self, are especially important during your healing journey from infidelity. Richard J. Foster (1992), author of *Prayer: Finding the Heart's True Home*, noted that prayers of petition are like "our staple diet" (p. 179). In other words, petitions to God are like bread and water for our spiritual nutrition. Foster (1992) further suggested that we should not erroneously confuse spiritual maturity with the increase in prayers of praise and decrease in petitionary prayers. We should refrain from seeing our personal requests as petty or selfish, for God is always interested in what we have to say. Fundamental to our relationship with God is the element of asking. Jesus said,

"Ask and it will be given to you; seek and you will find; knock and the door will be opened to you. For everyone who asks receives; he who seeks finds; and to him who knocks the door will be opened" (Matthew 7:7-8 NIV).

To reiterate, no prayer is ever unworthy. God sees each person as significant and each prayer as a treasure. In fact, he values you and your prayers so much that he would leave ninety-nine behind just to look for you if you were lost.

See that you do not look down on one of these little ones. For I tell you that their angels in heaven always see the face of my Father in Heaven. What do you think? If a man owns a hundred sheep, and one of them wanders away, will he not leave the ninety-nine on the hills and go to look for the one that wandered off? And if he finds it, I tell you the truth, he is happier about that one sheep than about the ninety-nine that did not wander off. In the same way your Father in heaven is not willing that any of these little ones should be lost (Matthew 18:10-14 NIV).

Asking for specific prayer requests accomplishes several things: it strengthens your personal relationship with God; it sustains the hierarchy of Father and child between God and you, reinforcing your dependence on Him; it allows God an opportunity to delightfully, generously, and mercifully give to one of His children; and it validates your feelings and needs. (Validation is especially important following discovery of infidelity when egos are bruised and self-esteem is often fragile and compromised.)

One betrayed spouse used to pray against the A's when she was married. She would talk to God and ask Him to protect her marriage from: **A**dultery, **A**ddiction, **A**nger, and **A**rguing. When she learned her husband had been unfaithful, she was confused by God's lack of intervention since she had specifically prayed against **A**dultery. She just knew her prayers would be in line with His will. How could He say no to such a lovely prayer?

We must acknowledge and not be blind to the issue of unanswered prayers, said Foster (1992). Sometimes things are not meant to be understood and we must come to accept this, although difficult and agonizing. We repeatedly ask ourselves the timeless questions about why atrocities of war, crime, famine, sexual abuse, disease, adultery, etc. occur, despite fervent prayers happening across the world. We often create theories in an attempt to psychologically understand the helpless "whys" of unnecessary (at least in our view) pain and suffering. At other times, the reason for suffering remains so mysterious and illogical that we are left purely to conclude that the explanation can only be revealed when we reach heaven and can ask God Himself. In the meantime, we must rely on faith in God that His power, care, and love are sufficient to see us through life. "And the peace of God which transcends all understanding will guard your hearts and your minds in Christ Jesus" (Philippians 4:7 NIV).

God's Will

Leslie Weatherhead (1944), author of *The Will of God*, delineates God's will into three types: God's intentional will, God's circumstantial will, and God's ultimate, transforming will. Additionally, God gave us the powerful gift of free will to make our own individual choices in life, which may or may not be in line with His intentional will. This concept of free will is beyond the scope of this book, but is a fascinating topic for further discussion and study. I include these terms about will in this section regarding prayer because it is helpful in understanding the outcome of prayers and how God responds to our prayers.

Intentional will, as Weatherhead (1944) described it, is the ideal purpose of God; what he originally designed or intended. His intentional will is always love-based, and never includes evil, sorrow, heartbreak, sickness, or suffering. Second, God's circumstantial will is when the evil of man brings about circumstances that are incongruent with God's plan and He relinquishes his original design *temporarily* as He gives us the gift of free will to make our own choices (Weatherhead, 1944). Third, God's ultimate will is the transformation of circumstantial will back to God's original design (Weatherhead, 1944). No amount of evil or suffering can prevent the transformation of God's circumstantial will back to His ultimate will. The death and resurrection of Christ is the most poignant example of God's redeeming plan to restore His original intent.

Understanding the will of God helps us to realize that infidelity was not in His original, intentional will. Circumstances brought about by man create the chaos and painful consequences of infidelity.

However, the exciting hope to cling to is that God has the power and can transform circumstances to realign with His original plan, as we rely on Him in trust.

Prayer is a perfect example of how God is the ultimate alchemist at work. In literal terms, alchemy is the process of transforming something raw, such as the base metal of iron, into pure gold. Metaphorically speaking, God, as an alchemist, has the power to transform our hurt and pain to reveal His glory. He is often working audaciously in the spotlight, or sometimes subtly behind the scenes, transforming our pain and suffering; salving our wounds, and comforting and mending our broken hearts and shattered dreams.

In trying to understand why God permitted adultery in her marriage despite her fervent prayers against it, one betrayed spouse developed her own set of theories as to what God might have been thinking. The theories ranged from a simple "no," because He is God and can answer the way He chooses, and other theories involved her purification and refinement or duties for His kingdom. The following were her theories:

- No.
- Not now.
- Not in this marriage.
- I have other plans for you.
- I want to see how you use infidelity to further My kingdom.
- I want you to minister to other people in pain and you need this difficult education and refining. I promise to be with you the whole way.
- I love you so much and want to draw you closer to Me. Pain often has this effect.
- You need an opportunity to display the art and gifts of forgiveness and humility. I will show you how.

Our God is freely giving and generous. He is all-knowing, powerful, omniscient, and loving. He is known as the God who gives and takes away.

Gives	Takes Away
... The LORD is able to **give** thee much more than this. II Chronicles 25:9 KJV And I will **give** unto thee the keys of the kingdom of heaven . . . Matthew 16:19 KJV And I **give** unto them eternal life and they shall never perish, neither shall any man pluck them out of my hand. John 10:28 KJV For the LORD God is a sun and shield: the LORD will **give** grace and glory: no good thing will he withhold from them that walk uprightly. Psalm 84:11 KJV	He will swallow up death in victory; and the Lord God will wipe away tears from off all faces; and the rebuke of his people shall he **take away** from off all the earth: for the LORD hath spoken. Isaiah 25:8 KJV By this therefore shall the iniquity of Jacob be purged; and this is all the fruit to **take away** his sin . . . Isaiah 27:9 KJV And ye know that he was manifested to **take away** our sins; and in him is no sin. I John 3:5 KJV

Although some prayers get answered and some do not, some purposes for suffering are revealed and some are not, what we know for certain is that Jesus understood and understands perfectly what an unanswered prayer felt and feels like. He can empathize with our pain in all dimensions. He prayed to God while in excruciating pain on the cross, "Eloi, Eloi, lama sabachthani?" Translated, this means, "My God, my God, why have you forsaken me?" (Matthew 27:46 NIV) Foster(1992) encouraged that we can rest assured that we have a redeemer who in the midst of His pain of crucifixion, experienced the anguish of unanswered prayer and empathizes with our confusion of "Why?"

Intercessory Prayer

Intercessory prayers, those defined as lifting requests up to God to intercede for the desires and needs of others, are also healing for the one praying. Praying for others helps strengthen our personal relationships with loved ones. Additionally, it teaches us to rely on God as we lift up our cherished prayer requests for those whom we love the most. Moreover, lifting up intercessory prayer fosters our own healing as we ask God to bless and love others. Jesus said the second greatest Commandment is, "Love your neighbor as yourself" (Matthew 22:39 NIV). Praying for others is a way to love them. Intercessory prayer is a gift to others which can also help us move through our own hardships or times of pain. For example, one individual was undergoing medical treatment and it required much testing with various scans. A bit claustrophobic, she developed her own strategy to manage her anxiety about being confined while in the MRI tube. She decided she would pray for others, beginning with the letter A in the alphabet and continuing letter by letter. She reported that she only got to the letter E by the time the scan was over, but added J to include her son. This is a perfect example of how intercessory prayer can act as a tool to help move us through difficult times of anxiety, pain, or suffering. She had used prayer to help distract her from her anxiety, get her mind off her own problems, and instead focus on blessing others.

Additionally, intercessory prayer provides the betrayed spouse an opportunity to pray for the straying spouse. It is especially important to challenge yourself to pray prayers of intercession during times of hurt and anger because they help facilitate forgiveness. By praying *for* the straying spouse, the intercessory prayer actually decreases the hurt, anger, or bitterness inside of you, beginning the transformation process to compassion and forgiveness. Although prayers for the straying spouse may feel counterintuitive during periods of anger, challenge yourself to pray one thing per day for your straying spouse, no matter how small. Prayer is another one of God's healing and purifying processes which has a special transforming power. We can pray for others just as Christ role modeled the ultimate intercessory sacrifice for us.

Therefore I will give him a portion among the great, and he will divide the spoils with the strong, because he poured out his life unto death, and was numbered with the transgressors. For he bore the sin of many, and made intercession for the transgressors (Isaiah 53:12 NIV).

Counseling

Counseling (also called therapy) is an important part of healing after an affair. Couples counseling is essential for healthy reconciliation and individual counseling is helpful to aid in personal healing for both the betrayed and straying spouses. It is important to seek the advice of others when you or your marriage is in crisis. Through an objective lens, a trained professional can observe things about you or your relationship that you cannot see. Thus, it is important to seek out the counsel from a minister (a pastoral counselor) or a mental health professional (a psychiatrist, a licensed psychologist, a licensed professional counselor, a licensed clinical social worker, or a licensed marriage and family therapist). scripture teaches us the importance of seeking counsel.

- ... Come now therefore, and let us take counsel together. Nehemiah 6:7 KJV
- We took sweet counsel together and walked unto the house of God in company. Psalm 55:14 KJV
- Where no counsel is, the people fall: but in the multitude of counsellors there is safety. Proverbs 11:14 KJV
- The way of a fool is right in his own eyes: but he that hearkeneth unto counsel is wise. Proverbs 12:5 KJV

Counseling helps assess for mistaken beliefs or distorted thinking and evaluates for mental health symptoms, such as depression, anxiety, or post traumatic stress. Counseling teaches new coping strategies for problems, helps with decision-making and goal setting, and provides appropriate medication or community referrals when necessary.

Choosing a Counselor

Choosing a counselor or therapist is a significant and personal process. It is not uncommon to try several providers before finding the "right fit." It is important that the therapeutic relationship feels "right," as opposed to trying to be a "good patient" and forcing it to work. Age, gender, years of experience, clinical areas of interest, personality style, and theoretical orientation are things to consider when selecting your therapist. It is most important that you feel confident in your therapist's skill set, feel safe and comfortable with your therapist, feel an absence of judgment from your therapist, and be willing to be honest and transparent in your sessions. It is imperative to find a therapist with a marriage counseling specialty; infidelity experience would be ideal. If you have a healthcare plan, you may contact the mental health vendor and ask specifically for a therapist with an infidelity specialty. Therapists typically list their areas of interest with health insurance companies for referral purposes. Another helpful resource in choosing a therapist with infidelity experience is the website developed by renowned author Peggy Vaughan, who has written multiple self-help resources on infidelity. (www.dearpeggy.com) On this site, recommended therapists with infidelity experience are listed by state and city.

Medication

Discovery of infidelity can often trigger depressive episodes or anxiety attacks in the betrayed spouse or straying spouse, too. Because discovery can be so traumatic, it is not unusual for symptoms to develop because the body is overwhelmed and responding to a crisis situation. Most symptoms are episodic, or temporary, unless there is a previously underlying condition that could be exacerbated. Symptoms are addressed with therapy, medication, and good self-care. Symptoms of depression to look for include:

- Depressed mood (feeling down, blue, sad)
- Sleep disturbance (trouble falling or staying asleep, early morning awakenings)
- Appetite changes or weight changes
- Feelings of hopelessness or helplessness
- Crying spells
- Low energy, fatigue
- Low motivation
- Suicidal thoughts
- Preoccupation with death or dying

- Anhedonia (lack of pleasure or enjoyment in activities that previously brought about joy)
- Apathy, listlessness

Symptoms of anxiety to look for include:

- Feeling anxious or nervous
- Feeling frightened or scared
- Feeling afraid something bad will happen
- Shortness of breath
- Chest pain or tightness
- Racing or pounding heart
- Sweaty palms
- Agitation
- Muscle tightness or tension
- Lump in the throat
- Butterflies in the stomach

If you have any of the above symptoms of depression or anxiety and they are interfering with your daily functioning, please seek medical attention to determine if you can benefit from the aid of a medication. Antidepressants are available for depression symptoms and anti-anxiety medications help relieve anxiety symptoms. Important questions to ask your physician about medication:

- How does the medication work?
- Is the medication habit-forming (addictive)?
- What symptoms does it address?
- What are common side effects?
- How long will it take to achieve results?
- How long will I have to take the medication(s)?
- Are there any drug interactions with my other medications?
- How much does it cost?

Case examples

Tania learned her husband of four years had been having several affairs. She reported feeling heartbroken and devastated. She began to have trouble falling asleep at night, as she would obsess about the affairs. This led to sleep deprivation, loss of appetite, depressed mood, and loss of motivation, as she spent most of her time on the couch crying and "watching mindless television" during the day. She had little energy to take care of herself and the house. Missing two commitments finally led her to seek medical attention when she realized the symptoms were interfering with her health and relationships. She sought the counsel of a therapist, who referred her to a psychiatrist who prescribed an antidepressant for her. She began to feel better after a few weeks and started seeing the counselor regularly to process her hurt from her husband's affairs.

Katelyn, a thirty-two-year-old restaurant manager, began immediately having anxiety symptoms after her husband revealed his six-month affair to her. One day at work, she experienced severe anxiety, shortness of breath, racing and pounding heart, tremors, and sweating. Not realizing what was going on, she and her coworkers mistook the symptoms for a heart attack (anxiety symptoms often mimic a heart attack), and called 911. She rode in an ambulance to the ER, where the physician accurately diagnosed an anxiety attack after all medical tests were cleared for her heart. The doctor recommended anti-anxiety medication and some therapy. Katelyn agreed and got into treatment to begin processing her husband's affair.

Exercise

Most of us have heard at some time or another that exercise is a good remedy for stress. This, in fact, is true. Research heavily favors exercise for numerous health and wellness benefits. God made our bodies to need and thrive on physical activity. He made us exceptionally well. "For you created my innermost being; you knit me together in my mother's womb. I praise you because I am fearfully and wonderfully made; your works are wonderful, I know that full well" (Psalm 139:13-14 NIV). Exercise will help you cope with stress, feel better physically, and feel better emotionally. Paul, when writing to the church in the Greek city of Corinth, said to honor God by treating the body well and metaphorically defined the body as a special, sacred place like a temple.

"Do you not know that your body is a temple of the Holy Spirit, who is in you, whom you have received from God? You are not your own; you were bought at a price. Therefore honor God with your body" (I Corinthians 6:19-20 NIV).

Benefits of exercise include:

- Improved mood
- Increased energy level
- Regulated sleep
- Improved stamina
- Improved muscle tone
- Improved physical and emotional strength
- Improved self-esteem
- Distraction from stressful situations
- Improved overall health functioning and immunity
- Weight loss
- Reduction in the level of cortisol, the stress hormone

If you are already exercising, continue to perform your exercise routine. If you are not exercising, challenge yourself to slowly build up by starting with ten minutes of walking, jogging, or swimming or another favored activity each day. Try to select an activity you will find some enjoyment in, for example, walking in a lovely park or neighborhood and enjoying nature. Exercise that is enjoyable is more likely to be incorporated into your lifestyle versus being used as a temporary crisis management strategy. Avoid over exercising or doing too much at once for this can result in injury. If you have medical problems or back or pain issues, talk to your physician about what type of exercise will be helpful and safe for you.

I want to encourage you. Remember that anyone can do anything for ten minutes. Use every step, every stroke, each repetition, or each lap to symbolize that you are getting stronger. One woman used each step she walked to symbolize pounding out her anger about her husband's affairs. She wanted to get it out each day before he got home so she would be less likely to take it out on him. It was her way of transforming her anger toward forgiveness.

Journaling

Journaling is a healing coping skill that allows a betrayed spouse to write out thoughts and feelings in a personal and private way. There is no distinct or incorrect way to journal. In other words, there is no right or wrong way to journal. Journal entries can be disjointed and grammatically incorrect, or written in code, poetry or lyrical format. Some journalists write letters to God, while others write long narratives to themselves and others or draw pictures. Still others write daily scripts about the day's events, whereas some relay the emotional aspects of their deepest, darkest pain.

Most journaling is subjective to its author, although it can have some guidelines. For example, structured journaling is writing about a specific topic, assigned perhaps by a therapist. This is the opposite of unstructured journaling, otherwise known as free-association journaling, which is writing about whatever comes to mind.

Journaling has a unique therapeutic and transforming nature. In a most inexplicable way, getting one's thoughts out on paper helps one feel better. It can be cathartic. One woman described journaling as a "release" for her. Even though she was not in control of her husband's affairs, she felt more at peace after writing out her thoughts and feelings. Here is an excerpt from her journal:

May 10th
Dear God,

I praise you always! I come to you in sorrow. Please change me. I want to learn and grow as I ask these things of you. I am having trouble forgiving my husband for various things. I feel flooded with many feelings—hurt, betrayal, anger, pain. I pray that he would learn to say kinder things and be more discerning with his tongue. I pray that I would be more resilient to his words and take them less personally or literally. I pray that he would not have a desire to stay out past midnight. I pray that you would curb his appetite for alcohol and protect him from drinking and driving and always keep him safe. I pray that he would not have a penchant for pornography, but have a desire for me only. Please, Lord, convict him to refuse lust for other women. I pray, Lord, that you surround him with positive, healthy, pure friends who know You, who can be a spiritual influence on him. Shape me, Lord. Prevent me from being judgmental, but help me to be salt and light, role-modeling your ways to others. Help my thoughts be pure and in line with Your will. Please help me with my depression. Please help me find the right match with a counselor. I am so looking forward to the prayer group on

Wednesday night to hear what You have to say. Please give me the strength and courage to go to Al-Anon and help me learn healthy coping skills and boundaries. Give me discernment and clarity about future plans for a family.

Love, Rebecca

Angela wrote in her journal in a structured way, evaluating each day following the discovery of her husband's affair. She used her own ranking system (1-10). One equaled a good day and ten signified a terrible day. Because she had a history of depression, she also logged if she took her medication and exercised so she could keep track of her coping skills. Because she was quick to intervene with good self-care (medication, therapy, journaling, and exercise), she was able to manage her depression symptoms despite her difficult crisis situation. This does not mean she did not suffer, for it would be inhuman not to suffer after the discovery of an affair, but she was able to maintain her functioning despite her diagnosis of depression.

Angela's journal:

JUNE 6—RETT DISCLOSED HE HAD AFFAIR WITH SECRETARY. SHE IS TWENTY-FOUR YEARS OLD; FEELING SICK, SHOCK, NUMB

FORGOT MEDS   EXERCISE: NO

TODAY: 10

JUNE 7—CALLED THERAPIST, BUT SHE IS FULL UNTIL NEXT WEEK; GOT ON CANCEL LIST; FEELING SICK, NO APPETITE, DEPRESSED; WONDERING WHAT MISTRESS LOOKS LIKE; WHY?

MEDS: YES   EXERCISE: YES

TODAY: 10

JUNE 8—FEELING DEPRESSED, QUESTIONING SELF, BODY IMAGE; WONDERING IF I SHOULD CALL HIS SECRETARY AND TELL HER OFF

MEDS: YES   EXERCISE: NO

TODAY: 9

JUNE 9—WENT TO SEE THERAPIST—FELT BETTER AFTER TALKING ABOUT THE AFFAIR; SHE WAS IN AS MUCH SHOCK AS I WAS; FEELS GOOD TO TALK ABOUT IT; TALKED ABOUT TEMPORARILY INCREASING MY MEDS; WILL SEE M.D. NEXT WEEK

MEDS: YES   EXERCISE: NO

TODAY: 7

JUNE 10—TALKED TO RETT ABOUT THE AFFAIR, BUT HE IS RELUCTANT TO ANSWER MY QUESTIONS; THIS MAKES ME SUSPICIOUS; I DON'T LIKE HIM WORKING WITH HER; BAD DAY—GOT INTO A FIGHT—HE SLEPT UPSTAIRS AND I CRIED ALL NIGHT

MEDS: YES   EXERCISE: YES

TODAY: 10

JUNE 11—RETT AGREED TO GO TO COUNSELING WITH ME. THAT MAKES ME FEEL MORE HOPEFUL. I STILL FEEL ANXIOUS ALL DAY WHEN HE IS AT WORK—FIND MYSELF WANTING HIM TO CALL ME 20X A DAY SO HE IS PAYING ATTENTION TO ME AND NOT HER

MEDS: YES   EXERCISE: YES

TODAY: 8

JUNE 12—WENT TO DINNER TOGETHER AND RETT BOUGHT FLOWERS FOR ME; HASN'T DONE THAT IN THREE YEARS. HE CRIED FOR THE FIRST TIME. HE SAID HE WILL LOOK FOR A NEW JOB

MEDS: YES   EXERCISE: NO

TODAY: 5

JUNE 13—STILL CAN'T BELIEVE THIS IS HAPPENING TO US; I THOUGHT WE WERE A HAPPY COUPLE—STARTING TO FEEL VERY ANGRY AT RETT FOR ALL HIS LYING. GOING TO GET TESTED FOR STDS TODAY—HOW EMBARRASSING—HOPE THE NURSE DOESN'T THINK I AM A WHORE

MEDS: YES   EXERCISE: YES

TODAY: 8

Support Groups

Joining an infidelity support group is fundamental to healing after discovery of a spouse's affair. Beyond Affairs Network (BAN) was established in 1980 by Peggy Vaughan, author of *Beyond Affairs*, after she went public about her personal story of her husband's affair. At the writing of this book, BAN has expanded internationally to include multiple support groups in thirteen countries in the world. Domestically, it houses eighty-six support groups in the United States and nine in Canada. BAN support groups are for the support and healing of the betrayed spouse.

In 2006, Peggy Vaughan turned her directorship over to Anne and Brian Bercht, co-authors of *My Husband's Affair Became the Best Thing That Ever Happened to Me*. Information about BAN support groups can also be accessed through the website www.beyondaffairs. com. If you reside in a city that does not have a support group, you can listen to free teleconferences through the website. Furthermore, Anne and Brian Bercht lead therapeutic seminars through their organization, Passionate Life, offering affair recovery programs for couples seeking reconciliation and healing weekend retreats for the betrayed spouse.

Support group attendance is liberating, because it lets you know that you are not the only one in your situation. You will begin to bond with the other group members while you hear their stories. Revealing your story and listening to others is cathartic and you will identify with the dynamics being shared. This phenomenon is called group cohesion and it is therapeutic to become one of a group when enduring pain. Please know you do not have to endure the struggle of infidelity alone. Bell (2007) noted there is a "universal sisterhood" among women who have been cheated on, for they all have broken hearts in common. Being around others who can empathize with the pain of infidelity can be helpful.

Furthermore, while attending a support group you can become educated about affairs in general, techniques to help in affair recovery, and you can receive recommendations about helpful reading materials. BAN groups often provide supportive, educational information and provide teaching on anger, forgiveness, obsessive thinking, and the affair partner. The topics can be very helpful for education and healing.

Betrayed spouses noted some of the most insightful and therapeutic tips they received came from BAN meetings.

Support groups are also a way to make new friendships with others. Social support is imperative when going through a crisis such as infidelity. Having a friend who understands the dynamics and implications of infidelity can be a bonus. The name "support groups" describes their purpose: to strengthen, to join together, and to build one another up. The Bible says, "In him the whole building is joined together and rises to become a holy temple in the Lord. And in him you too are being built together to become a dwelling place in which God lives by his Spirit" (Ephesians 2:21-22 NIV). This scriptural passage refers to the church, which is meant to provide strength and support to its members, although some churches do this better than others. Support groups model this function of the fellowship of the church.

Bibliotherapy

My recommendation is to read as many books about infidelity as you can to arm yourself with information. Some you will like and some you will not. You can incorporate the helpful information and discard the unhelpful. Perhaps you will glean some valuable nugget from each book you read. A reference list is provided in the back of this book as a starting place for your recommended reading.

Reading the Bible is also a good source of hope and encouragement. The Bible is full of stories of individuals who have been through the types of pain that you are going through. Biblical figures have experienced adultery, war, incest, infertility, murder, fear, loss, death, grief, sickness, and much more. The Bible also provides hope and encouragement alongside the pain. Although pain and suffering will be a part of our lives from time to time, they will be temporary. There is a time for pain, yet there is a time for celebration and joy, too.

> To everything there is a season, and a time to every purpose under the heaven: A time to be born, and a time to die; a time to plant, and a time to pluck up that which is planted; A time to kill, and a time to heal; a time to break down, and a time to build up; A time to weep, and a time to laugh; a time to mourn, and a time to dance; A time to cast away stones, and a time to gather stones together,

and a time to embrace, and a time to refrain from embracing; A
time to get, and a time to lose; a time to keep, and a time to cast
away; A time to rend, and a time to sew; a time to keep silence and
a time to speak; A time to love, and a time to hate; a time of war,
and a time of peace (Ecclesiastes 3:1-8 KJV).

Nurturing Activities

Nurturing activities are behavioral activities in which you engage that
nurture, feed, protect, support, encourage, and promote growth for the
self. They pamper you, delight you, and remind you that you are special,
good, and worthy of being treated kindly. Most betrayed spouses doubt
their self-esteem following the discovery of an affair. They often blame
themselves, question their body image, question their sexual appeal, or
their marital or parenting skills. Nurturing activities are to remind you
that the affair was NOT your fault and to help you re-build self-esteem
or conquer any self-doubt that has crept into your mind.

Nurturing activities also serve to combat the shame and humiliation
of the affair and to manage depression and anxiety symptoms. When
individuals are feeling depressed or anxious, they often forget to take
care of themselves. After the shock of the discovery of an affair, one
does not always think about self-nurturing, because the pain is all
encompassing. This section is to help you be more cognizant about the
special need to care for yourself during this critical time. Jesus nurtured
himself when He allowed expensive perfume to be poured on his body
prior to his execution. He knew He was about to encounter the extreme
pain of crucifixion so He chose to receive this nurturing gift of care
from a friend. Similarly, we can choose to nurture ourselves through
loving self-care and through the care and comfort of others.

> **Matthew's Gospel**
>
> **While Jesus was in Bethany in the home of a man known as
> Simon the Leper, a woman came to him with an alabaster jar
> of very expensive perfume, which she poured on his head as
> he was reclining at the table. When the disciples saw this,
> they were indignant. "Why this waste?" they asked, "This**

perfume could have been sold at a high price and the money given to the poor." Aware of this Jesus said to them, "Why are you bothering this woman? She has done a beautiful thing to me. The poor you will always have with you, but you will not always have me. When she poured this perfume on my body, she did it to prepare me for burial. I tell you the truth, wherever this gospel is preached throughout the world, what she has done will also be told in memory of her."

Matthew 26:6–13 NIV

Mark's Gospel

While he was in Bethany, reclining at the table in the home of a man known as Simon the Leper, a woman came with an alabaster jar of very expensive perfume, made of pure nard. She broke the jar and poured the perfume on his head. Some of those present were saying indignantly to one another, "Why this waste of perfume? It could have been sold for more than a year's wages and the money given to the poor." And they rebuked her harshly. "Leave her alone," said Jesus. "Why are you bothering her? She has done a beautiful thing to me. The poor you will always have with you, and you can help them any time you want. But you will not always have me. She did what she could. She poured perfume on my body beforehand to prepare for my burial. I tell you the truth, wherever the gospel is preached throughout the world, what she has done will also be told, in memory of her."

Mark 14:3–9 NIV

To elaborate, nurturing activities are those that cherish, pamper, pleasure, delight, entertain, and indulge you in healthy ways. Nurturing activities are typically subjective and idiosyncratic, for different people favor different things. One way to think about ideas to nurture yourself is to focus on the five senses that God gave you: visual, auditory, gustatory (taste), olfactory (smell), and tactile (touch). The following are examples of nurturing activities from the five senses:

- **Visual**: Enjoy the different colors of a bouquet of flowers you buy for yourself
- **Auditory**: Listen to your favorite relaxing music
- **Gustatory**: Cook your favorite recipe or ask your spouse to cook it for you
- **Olfactory**: Light a scented candle and enjoy the aroma
- **Tactile**: Wrap up in your favorite soft blanket

Nurturing activities are there to remind you that you are loved during a time when you may feel most forsaken. You may be wondering if you will ever be loved again or wondering if you can ever love or trust again. This is the time when nurturing activities can be most valuable. Nurturing activities serve to indulge you and make you feel loved the way God intended. "The LORD appeared to us in the past saying: 'I have loved you with an everlasting love; I have drawn you with loving-kindness. I will build you up again and you will be rebuilt'" (Jeremiah 31:3-4 NIV).

Nurturing activities are *not* activities that have the potential to be detrimental or destructive. Because nurturing activities always promote growth, behaviors that are damaging or negative in any way are excluded. For example, if you are on a tight budget, it would be counterproductive to spend a lot of money buying new things for yourself. Stick to nurturing activities that are free or low-cost until your financial situation permits shopping. Furthermore, if you have a medical condition, such as diabetes or obesity, overindulging in a box of cookies or a bottle of wine will be disadvantageous for you. Think wisely when making food choices. Indulging from time to time is okay, but overindulging is unhealthy and not nurturing. Please see a list of one-hundred nurturing activities in Appendix A at the end of the book.

Discussion Questions

1. How will you use prayer during your healing journey?
2. Are you willing to pray *for* the straying spouse?
3. Will you or have you pursued counseling with a professional?
4. Do you or did you need the aid of medication after discovering your spouse's affair?
5. How can you incorporate exercise into your healing plan?

CHAPTER 11

RECOVERY AND AFFAIR-PREVENTION

Although frequently used, the trendy psychobabble phrase "affair-proof" is a bit of a misnomer. Affairs can happen to anyone and there is no guarantee against infidelity in relationships, however, there are several recommendations to help safeguard your marriage from affairs.

Reiterating Commitment

A good initial defense is an overall mutual agreement from both parties to vow to maintain honesty and faithfulness. I often have both spouses verbally contract to faithfulness and to cease any extramarital relationships before beginning couples work together after I learn there has been infidelity. Some couples choose to formally renew their vows at a ceremony following infidelity, while others take a trip to symbolize reiteration of their verbally-renewed commitment. You can be creative in how you choose to renew your commitment with one another.

Additionally, make a couples' mission statement for the marriage. Outline what you and your spouse desire to accomplish with your renewed relationship and include monogamy in the mission. Without a common mission, intimacy is rarely achieved. Reiterating commitment and establishing a marriage mission statement require the fundamental belief that infidelity is unhealthy. Adam Hamilton (2004) in his book, *Making Marriage Last a Lifetime: Biblical Principals on Love, Marriage, and Sex*, suggested that individuals should have the core belief that "adultery is not God's will."

Communication

Second, talk openly about the affair. Effective communication requires maturity, empathy, and patience on the straying spouse's part. The straying spouse will need to be willing to answer questions as long as the betrayed spouse has questions. This willingness and openness is imperative to the healing process of the marriage. The more openness demonstrated in the beginning, the more quickly healing takes place. If straying spouses are hesitant or reluctant to discuss the affair, it appears as if they are hiding information or continuing to keep secrets, and this is detrimental to the trust-rebuilding process. Although conversations about the affair can be uncomfortable and painful, they will lessen in frequency and duration over time if you initially discuss and confront them.

Counseling

Third, go to counseling. Seeking couples therapy is imperative to the health and integrity of a relationship after an affair. Couples can learn better communication skills, assess problem areas in the marriage, address vulnerability factors, and discuss trust-rebuilding strategies. The straying spouse must prove himself over time with honesty, consistency, and trustworthy behaviors. In other words, trust is: **proven behavior over time**. Therapy is a way for the straying spouse to be accountable with specific goals. On the flip side, the betrayed spouse has to learn to trust again and demonstrate compassion and forgiveness. She is working on a completely different agenda than the straying spouse. Therapy is a way for her to be accountable for her anger. She can check in with the therapist to see how she is progressing toward forgiveness and compassion toward the straying spouse. Furthermore, much like a car cannot run without gas or oil, a marriage needs tune ups from time to time. We get our oil changed every three months, and our teeth cleaned twice a year. Some people get their hair colored every six weeks. Why don't we treat our marriages like our car, our teeth, or our hair? I recommend therapy for troubled marriages, especially those that are in crisis because of infidelity. Then, participate in maintenance therapy after the crisis is over . . . just to check in.

Assess Vulnerability Factors

It is important to assess personal and marital vulnerability factors regularly. Know what the limitations and weaknesses are in the marriage that led up to the infidelity. Keep a watchful eye on those issues. Write them down on a list and place them in plain view so you will not be tempted to avoid or overlook them. Some vulnerability factors preceding or occurring during the affair might have been temporary and may no longer be present (i.e., short term financial strain due to a job loss). If this is the case, they can be taken off the list. Other vulnerability factors can be long-term or permanent issues, such as medical conditions or family history of affairs. The long-term or permanent vulnerability issues need to stay on your visible list. Your therapist can help you understand more about classification of vulnerability issues. Moreover, it is important to schedule weekly discussions at home, in addition to therapy sessions, to talk about current vulnerability factors. These conversations help keep lines of communication open and strengthen the integrity of the marital relationship to help prevent future affairs.

Worship and Prayer

There is nothing more strengthening than praying and worshiping together to fortify a marriage. God loves seeing His beloved children band together to praise Him or petition Him. "For where two or three are gathered together in my name, there am I in the midst of them" (Matthew 18:20 KJV).

Praying together helps draw couples closer together and closer to God. Praying keeps you in tune with one another's needs and desires and with the ultimate source of meeting those needs. Sit together and hold hands when you pray, increasing your affection and physical connection.

Worshiping together shows your united purpose as a couple in serving the Lord. "Praise the Lord. I will extol the LORD with all my heart in the council of the upright and in the assembly" (Psalm 111:1 NIV). Attending church together helps facilitate Christian fellowship with others, provides service and mission opportunities, and allows for biblical learning, all of which strengthen the moral foundation on which love and commitment rest.

Accountability

Having an accountability plan after an affair is a way to safeguard and protect your marriage. Finding an accountability partner and joining an accountability group are two specific ways to increase security in a marriage that has suffered an affair. If reconciliation is the desired result, I believe that each member of the marriage after infidelity needs to find an accountability partner and join a group. The frequency of group attendance may be dissimilar depending on the needs of each person. Issues discussed may also be radically different for the betrayed spouse and the straying spouse. For example, the straying spouse may need to meet more frequently with his accountability partner in the beginning of recovery to demonstrate commitment to the marriage and to discuss sexual temptation prevention strategies. On the other hand, the betrayed spouse may need to discuss compassion techniques and steps for forgiveness. If she finds herself having difficulty being vulnerable to anxiety, fear, anger, or the need to police her straying spouse again, she may need to call her accountability partner and meet more frequently.

Start by finding an accountability partner who values monogamy and who will sponsor your pursuit of faithfulness in your marriage. Good accountability partners are sober, wise, mature individuals who are willing to be honest and confront unhealthy behaviors. Start by asking your minister or church elder who might be a good referral. Next, ask if accountability groups are available at your church. If not, you might consider starting one. Speaking with others who seek to safeguard the monogamy in their marriages is helpful for reducing the chance of an affair. Being around others who are like-minded is essential for encouraging one's growth in faithfulness.

Bust the Lust

Ed Young (2004) in his book, *Fatal Distractions*, encouraged the use of "lust-busters" as he warns against the destructive nature of sin and invites us all to live above life's fatal distractions. Young (2004) advocated examining and screening your media consumption as an accountability measure. In other words, protect your eyes and ears from incorporating destructive and tempting material. "I made a covenant with mine eyes: why then should I think upon a maid?" (Job 31:1 KJV) Be careful what you read, watch on TV or what movies you see, what kind of music you listen to, and what kind of places you frequent. In this sense, protect yourself as you would a precious, innocent child because illicit images and ideas regarding sex often stimulate illicit desires . . . which can become illicit behavior.

Bell (2007) noted that lust is the force that compels us to do scary things, occupies much of our psychological energy, and makes us unhappy. In other words, lust is the antecedent for destructive behavior and it causes turmoil. Acting out lust never generates positive outcomes. Bell (2007) wrote that lust can be enslaving, is always built on falsehood, never completely satiates, and never redeems its promise to provide.

Young (2004) also encouraged his readers to reflect upon the possible consequences of lustful thinking and behaving. Ask yourself *"Is a moment of sexual pleasure worth all the pain and heartache that could transpire?"* In other words, **think before you act**. "Then when lust hath conceived, it bringeth forth sin: and sin, when it is finished, bringeth forth death" (James 1:15 KJV). Hamilton (2004) suggested that, although sexual attraction to someone besides your spouse is normal, it is dangerous to fantasize about an affair, for the more thought given to the fantasies, the more likely it will lead to destructive action. In addition to the safeguard of **thinking before acting**, also monitor how much of your time is occupied with sexual fantasies involving someone besides your spouse. Practice restraint by removing these unwanted and unhealthy fantasies. The art of demonstrating restraint or refraining from immediate gratification is a sign of a mature marriage partner.

Discuss Attractions to Other Individuals with Your Spouse

All people have attractions to other individuals outside of the marriage. The key to preserving fidelity is to keep luring feelings at the benign level of attraction; that is, noticing others' attractiveness but choosing not to indulge this interest. Identifying warning signs (the desire to make eye contact, flirt, share personal information, spend time together, etc.) and preventing these behaviors or correcting any that have occurred are important for preventing an affair. Recognizing warning signs when they are still at the "desire" level, before they become actions, is mature affair-prevention. An attraction is harder to break once it has been indulged with action.

After infidelity, the reconciling couple must make a pact to discuss with one another any attractions they may have to other individuals. This form of healthy, safeguarding communication is a good habit in which to participate, even if your marriage has not suffered the devastating consequences of an affair. Although sharing with your spouse the feelings of attraction to another may sound like a terrifying proposition, even a fragile marriage can tolerate a discussion about an attraction to another individual much more easily than it can tolerate experiencing an affair.

This skill requires a planned commitment from each party, a high level of maturity and willingness from each person, and ideally, routinely scheduled discussions. One of my patients asked for some affair-prevention advice and this proposition was the idea I gave to her. She was horrified at the idea of discussing potential attractions to other people with her spouse and did not think she could tolerate it. Many people feel this way. This strategy is, again, best used when both people are in agreement and when the technique is routinely performed. Couples with higher levels of maturity can see the end result is open, safe communication and affair-prevention. It can be practiced by stating which celebrity or movie star you are most attracted to as a warm-up exercise. It is helpful to remember that just because you are attracted to another individual, does not mean you are going to act on it. The premise of this strategy is that *"If it is safe for me to talk about my attraction, I am less likely to act on it."* Ideally, each spouse's recognition of their own interest patterns toward the opposite sex will trigger them to put clear boundaries in place with anyone toward whom they feel an attraction. To clarify this idea, I warn you only to speak of these feelings to your spouse, *never* to the person to whom you are attracted. Even though most people have sexual attractions to someone outside the marriage at one time or another, Hamilton (2004) advised to *never* disclose the thoughts to the person, for the origin of an affair may begin with this perilous, preliminary disclosure.

Sex

Although most affairs do not occur because of lack of sex in the marriage, it is important to ensure that the sexual relationship is being nurtured. God made us sexual beings and sex is the sacred, covenant relationship that bonds husband and wife together. "My lover is mine and I am his . . . " (Song of Songs 2:16 NIV). God created the sexual experience of orgasm and He meant it to be only experienced in the marital bed. When sex is shared with others outside of the covenant marriage, hurt and destruction occur. Sex is a very powerful and sacred experience and it loses its strength when shared outside the marriage, for its power and mystery is drawn from its "exclusivity" (Bell, 2007).

Much like a fire confined to a fireplace provides warmth and comfort, a fire outside of the fireplace can be a dangerous and destructive conflagration.

Many people struggle to revive their sexual relationships after betrayal, for fear of being hurt again. Talk to one another about your concerns or fears about sexual issues and set a time to reconnect sexually. "Do not deprive each other except by mutual consent and for a time, so that you may devote yourselves to prayer. Then come together again so that Satan will not tempt you because of your lack of self control" (I Corinthians 7:5 NIV). Also, make time to have a date night once a week for courting and romance. When you go out together, refer to the time as a "date" to symbolize the romance and your special time together. "My lover spoke and said to me, 'Arise, my darling, my beautiful one and come with me . . . '"(Song of Songs 2:10 NIV).

Affair-Prevention in the Workplace

More affairs are originating in the workplace. Perhaps this is due to gender norms and technological advances that have changed over the past few decades in our work culture. First, more women are being educated than ever before, which places them in the workplace with men. The average age when people marry is rising, and many women are choosing to work on their careers before marrying and having children.

Second, business travel has increased, so flings or affairs are easier to conduct when away from home. Third, many work environments are mobile offices, so accountability is reduced. Since the introduction of the Internet, fewer people report to an office for a traditional nine-to-five job. Business can be conducted from any spot with a wireless connection. Without a requirement to be present or visible in the office, opportunities may arise where an individual might be more tempted to participate in an affair.

Individuals can establish goals and guidelines for themselves to help safeguard against being drawn into a workplace affair. First, if you are an employee and work with members of the opposite sex, have an accountability partner to help process any temptations or attractions you may be having. Second, make a commitment to always lunch in threes, never placing yourself in a position to be alone with someone of the opposite sex. Third, make a pact to never disclose any marital issues or personal problems with any member of the opposite sex at your workplace. Often unforeseen, this type of intimate disclosure can be a breeding ground for an affair. Fourth, make a commitment not to flirt with any member of the opposite sex at work if you or they are married. "Even a child is known by his doings, whether his work be pure, and whether it be right" (Proverbs 20:11 KJV).

If you are an employer, you have a wonderful opportunity to exercise your prestige and power in fighting the battle against infidelity. First, discourage interoffice dating with a formal policy. One man in my church stated that his employer had a formal policy that no two employees of the opposite sex could ride together in vehicles. This rule was essentially encouraging a "no dating" policy. He joked that he decided to ask the Director of Human Resources to lunch and she remarked, "You haven't read your employee handbook yet!" Additionally, emphasize the importance of senior employees role-modeling by following the rules and mentoring to junior employees or interns.

Second, host educational seminars conducted by a trained therapist teaching employees about the disadvantages and pitfalls of interoffice romances. Third, encourage each employee to have an employee adviser to aid with accountability. Fourth, have a no-penalty-for-honesty policy. Fifth, arrange projects, if possible, in threes, or encourage employees to schedule accountability sessions when trios are impossible.

Discussion Questions

1. After an affair, do you think reiterating and reestablishing commitment will be helpful for preventing future affairs?
2. What do you plan to do to secure your marriage from workplace vulnerabilities?
3. If reconciling, are you willing to discuss attractions to others with your spouse as an affair-prevention strategy?
4. If reconciling, are you and your spouse willing to pray and worship together?
5. If separating from your spouse, what specific affair-prevention strategies will you incorporate in a new relationship?

CHAPTER 12

FINDING THE SILVER LINING: THE "BENEFITS" OF INFIDELITY

I felt a twinge of incongruency as I was entitling this chapter. Much as, I suspect, my patients feel when I encourage them to welcome or embrace their pain as an opportunity for growth. It is hard to write or say the words "welcome" and "pain" or "benefit" and "infidelity" in the same sentence.

First let me be clear that I would never wish infidelity upon anyone. My ideal desire would be that all marriages remain blissfully and sacredly monogamous, which was and is God's original design. "Marriage should be honored by all, and the marriage bed kept pure, for God will judge the adulterer and all the sexually immoral" (Hebrews 13:4 NIV). However, we messed up God's original design with our unruly ways of behaving, so His perfect plan for marriage is not always realized.

One betrayed spouse noted her friends responded to her situation by saying she did not deserve to be cheated on. That is true, and then again, I don't think anyone *deserves* infidelity, even the most evil. It is not so much a matter of one being deserving, but more the fact that we live in a fallen world and don't get to choose our specific sufferings. What we do get to choose is how we react and respond to the often unintentional or unpredictable sufferings in our lives.

One benefit of infidelity is that it can highlight conflicts within an individual or in the marital relationship. Infidelity can be a catalyst for getting a couple into therapy to begin working on the relationship. The affair can be a vehicle for bringing out troublesome issues that need to be addressed in the marriage, or it can be an impetus for processing unresolved family of origin wounds that were impeding closeness in the marriage. A family of origin wound is an issue or hurt from one's childhood that he or she projects onto the marital relationship.

A second benefit of infidelity is that it typically forces more communication, fostering greater intimacy. I once had a woman tell me that her marriage was stronger after her husband's affair. Although this is not the case for all couples, it is more probable when couples seek therapy and are more willing to talk openly about the affair and affair-prevention.

The third advantage of affairs, or pain of any kind, is that suffering can be transformed into hope. Hope is **H**aving **O**ptimistic and **P**ositive **E**xpectations (HOPE). It just takes time. This is God, the redeemer of broken things, doing His most primitive work that reveals the most exquisite results.

> Not only so, but we also rejoice in our sufferings, because we know that suffering produces perseverance; perseverance, character; and character, hope. And hope does not disappoint us, because God has poured out his love into our hearts by the Holy Spirit, whom he has given us (Romans 5:3-5 NIV).

During her pain following discovery of infidelity, one betrayed spouse counted on the above verse and remained hopeful about how God would transform her suffering. She was curious to see what He would do to mend her shattered heart and what He is still doing to help with the healing journey. One thing that is important to remember is that you do not have to experience infidelity and its problems alone. In fact, God woos us closer to Him during times of difficulty. Many succumb to the delusion of self-sufficiency, and when the pain of infidelity hits, fall flat on their faces. The intensity of the pain can be a wake-up call to your own limitations and defenselessness, forcing you to look upward to God. In that sense, the pain of infidelity may turn out to be a blessing, a gift reminding you that you are not capable of living on your own without God, nor should you want to. In other words, the anguish many betrayed spouses endure allows them to draw closer to God and to be comforted and carried during a time when they may only be able to crawl. Utter dependence on God, thus fostering a deeper connection to Him, can be the "silver lining" that emerges from infidelity. I want to encourage you to maintain focus on the healing power of God and to remain eager and hopeful about how God will transform your suffering. Although the healing process is painful, keep your gaze fixated on God to see what He will reveal for you. Rest assured that you do not have to experience infidelity and its consequences alone. I want to boost your confidence that you shall be comforted and have your pain transformed. Remain hopeful always, for God does not disappoint.

- Therefore my heart is glad, and my glory rejoiceth: my flesh also shall rest in hope. Psalm 16:9 KJV
- "But now, Lord, what do I look for? My hope is in you." Psalm 39:7 NIV
- But for me, I will always have hope; I will praise you more and more. Psalm 71:14 NIV
- The LORD is good to those whose hope is in him, to the one who seeks him; Lamentations 3:25 NIV
- I pray also that the eyes of your heart may be enlightened in order that you may know the hope to which he has called you, the riches of his glorious inheritance in the saints . . . Ephesians 1:18 NIV

God has a plan of redemption and prosperity for each of us. He wants to give you hope and prosper you individually.

"For I know the plans I have for you," declares the LORD, "plans to prosper you and not to harm you, plans to give you hope and a future. Then you will call upon me and come and pray to me, and I will listen to you. You will seek me and find me when you seek me with all your heart. I will be found by you," declares the Lord, "and will bring you back from captivity . . . " (Jeremiah 29:11-13 NIV).

Another benefit of infidelity is that it gives betrayed spouses an opportunity to demonstrate mercy and forgiveness. Betrayed spouses often get sidetracked or fixated on the sinful behavior of straying spouses; however, the infidelity gifts you with an opportunity to become more Christlike and show mercy, compassion, and forgiveness. Although much like the straying spouse who does not change immediately, the betrayed spouse rarely shows the divine kind of immediate grace and forgiveness that God offers. However, the gift of infidelity challenges thinking to become more merciful, more understanding, and most of all, forgiving.

Additionally, as individuals develop and mature as Christians, it is through pain and afflictions that they have the treasure of becoming more and more in touch with who Christ really was and is. "And we, who with unveiled faces all reflect the Lord's glory, are being transformed into his likeness with ever-increasing glory, which comes from the Lord, who is the Spirit" (II Corinthians 3:18 NIV). Without our own tragedies and sufferings, we would be unable to empathize with the sanctification process (the process of becoming holy) and the magnitude of what it really implies when Jesus died a horrible death via crucifixion for our sins.

In addition to the valuable opportunity to become more Christlike by showing more mercy, compassion, and forgiveness, infidelity gives the betrayed spouse an occasion to demonstrate good character and witness for the Lord. Remember that you do not have control over most sufferings that occur in your life, but you always have the choice of how you will respond and react. Use the infidelity as an opportunity to role-model good character, ethics, and behavior to your children and others as you respond to your spouse. Use the infidelity as a chance to witness to friends about God's comfort and hope during painful times. Begin a support group for betrayed spouses, an accountability group, or a group for couples wanting to reconcile their marriages at your church or local community center. Join a BAN support group to role-model to friends and family the importance of speaking aloud about the affair. Remember that all can be a platform that reveal God's ability to trump pain and evil.

Role-modeling and displaying good and healthy behaviors will benefit you in the long run. Even though you never asked for or wanted the pain of infidelity, affairs provide an opportunity from which you can learn. It may require you to demonstrate responsibility, discipline, and delaying immediate gratification, tools revered by Peck (1978) when dealing with problems and pain. Never once have I heard a patient regret demonstrating responsibility, discipline, or delaying immediate gratification. If anything, they wish they would display these behaviors more frequently.

Although your life will be forever altered, because infidelity is a life-changing event, you may rest assured that your pain from infidelity will not last forever. To close this book, I leave you with one of my favorite verses for you to nestle close to your heart:

Thou hast turned for me my mourning into dancing . . . (Psalm 30:11 KJV)

Discussion Questions

1. What have you learned from your experience with infidelity?
2. What losses have you incurred from infidelity?
3. What gains have you experienced from infidelity?
4. What is one unexpected blessing from your encounter with infidelity?

Appendix A

100 NURTURING ACTIVITIES

1. Go to a coffee house and drink hot coffee
2. Read a book
3. Turn off your cell phone and the television for some quiet time
4. Feel yourself smile
5. Bake a dessert just for the smell
6. Dine at your favorite restaurant
7. Enjoy the colors of a flower bouquet that you buy for yourself
8. Listen to your favorite relaxing music
9. Wrap up in a soft blanket
10. Light a scented candle
11. Eat a piece of chocolate
12. Arrange for some time alone
13. Designate a chore-free day
14. Read a Bible story
15. Go outside and write down the first five sounds you hear
16. Put on your favorite pair of pajamas
17. Burn some incense
18. Make yourself a cup of hot tea
19. Go work out at the gym
20. Send yourself a card in the mail
21. Write a personal mission statement about caring for yourself
22. Go see a movie
23. Take a walk outside and pay attention to the sounds of the birds
24. Take a hot bubble bath or hot shower
25. Put fresh lavender or eucalyptus leaves in a vase
26. Have breakfast in bed
27. Take a nap
28. Paint your toenails a new, bright color

29. Practice how many different ways you can laugh
30. Lie on the grass outside and make shapes out of the clouds
31. Pick some flowers
32. Put lotion all over your body
33. Put scented oil in your bath
34. Have lunch with a friend
35. Buy a new outfit
36. Watch your favorite TV program uninterrupted
37. Think of your positive qualities that begin with the letter A, B, C, and all the way to Z
38. Try a new lipstick color
39. Listen to the laughter of children
40. Give yourself a facial
41. Sleep in
42. Bake a cake for yourself
43. Laugh out loud
44. Plan a vacation
45. Style or color your hair a new way
46. Have some quiet time for just you and God
47. Put some cedar chips in your closet or sweet-smelling sachets in your drawers
48. Take some photographs of something or someone you love
49. Call and talk to a friend
50. Get a manicure
51. Wear perfume or body spray
52. Eat fresh fruit
53. Have your eyebrows waxed or threaded
54. Make a wish aloud
55. Ask for a backrub from your partner
56. Go to a specialty bakery and select an item
57. Go to bed early
58. Take a walk in a nature preserve so you can be reminded how BIG God is and how capable He is of caring for you
59. Buy some of those soft, warm and fuzzy socks to wear
60. Wrap a present for yourself, then open it
61. Tell yourself, "I love you"
62. Pet a cat or dog
63. Treat yourself to an ice cream cone
64. Think positive things about yourself

65. Get a hot stone massage
66. Memorize a Bible passage about love, hope, or encouragement
67. Take time to visit a museum, exhibit, or event that you have been wanting to see
68. Try a new hobby
69. Write down your five best attributes
70. Sign up for a class
71. Check out books for pleasure at the library
72. Take a walk and look for butterflies
73. Write down ten of your favorite things
74. Drive somewhere new, just to check it out
75. In the winter, make ice cream out of the snow
76. Volunteer your time
77. Recite the phrase, "I am loveable" five times
78. Drink hot chocolate on a cold day
79. Make a craft project
80. Write a prayer on paper
81. Walk outside and feel the sunshine or wind on your face
82. Designate one hour of the day to represent "you" time
83. Meditate
84. Hire a babysitter
85. Play a game
86. Sing along with the radio
87. Pray for yourself
88. Pray for someone else
89. Plant flowers and watch them grow
90. Do some stretching
91. Sit by the warmth of a fire
92. For pet therapy, buy a goldfish to care for
93. Notice three things about nature when you are outside
94. Put a sticky note on your bathroom mirror reminding you to love yourself
95. Work a puzzle: crossword, jigsaw, or Sudoku
96. Try a new sport or athletic activity
97. Plant a tree to symbolize your healing
98. Try yoga
99. Bake some cookies
100. Do something nice for yourself "just because"

Appendix B

VULNERABILITY
FACTOR WORKSHEET

Directions:

List each factor in your marriage that could be a vulnerability factor to infidelity. Rate the vulnerability factors according to their type: short-term, long-term, or permanent.

Under each vulnerability factor, list goals to directly address the vulnerability factor.

Place this sheet somewhere visible where you will see it and be reminded daily of your goals.

Example:

Vulnerability factor: Job loss

Rating type: Short-term

Goals:

- Begin therapy immediately if job loss occurs to process grief, planning, and affair-prevention
- Maintain accountability group attendance during job search
- Begin career care group at church
- Always have resume updated
- Regularly attend networking lunches

Vulnerability
factor: _____

_____

Rating type:

_____

_____

Goals:

Vulnerability
factor: _____

_____

Rating type:

_____

_____

Goals:

REFERENCES

American Psychiatric Association. (2000). *Diagnostic and Statistical Manual of Mental Disorders.* (4th ed., text rev.). Washington DC: Author.

Bell, R. (2007). *Sex God: Exploring the Endless Connections Between Sexuality and Spirituality.* Grand Rapids, MI: Zondervan.

Brizendine, L. (2010). *The Male Brain: A Breakthrough Understanding of How Men and Boys Think.* New York, NY: Broadway Books.

Buss, D.M. (2000). *The Dangerous Passion: Why Jealousy Is as Necessary as Love and Sex.* New York, NY: The Free Press.

Carder, D. (1992). *Torn Asunder: Recovering from an Extramarital Affair.* Chicago, IL: Moody Publishers.

Earle, R. & Crow, G. (1989). *Lonely All the Time: Recognizing, Understanding and Overcoming Sex Addiction, for Addicts and Co-Dependents.* New York, NY: Pocket Books.

Foster, R.J. (1992). *Prayer: Finding the Heart's True Home.* New York: NY: Harper One.

Frankl, V. (1959). *Man's Search For Meaning.* Boston, MA: Beacon Press.

Gardner, T.A. (2002). *Sacred Sex: A Spiritual Celebration of Oneness in Marriage.* Colorado Springs, CO: Waterbrook Press.

Hamilton, A. (2004). *Making Love Last a Lifetime: Biblical Perspectives on Love, Marriage, and Sex.* Nashville, TN: Abingdon Press.

Lusterman, D. (1998). *Infidelity: A Survival Guide.* Oakland, CA: New Harbinger Publications, Inc.

Peck, M.S. (1978). *The Road Less Traveled.* New York, NY: Simon and Schuster.

Pittman, F. (1989). *Private Lies: Infidelity and the Betrayal of Intimacy.* New York, NY: W.W. Norton & Company.

Reill, P.H. & Wilson, E.J. (2004). *Encyclopedia of the Enlightenment.* (Rev. ed.). New York, NY: Facts on File, Inc.

Smith, T. (2003). *American Sexual Behavior—Trends, Socio-Demographic Differences and Risk Behavior.* (GSS Topical Report No. 25). University of Chicago: National Opinion Research Center.

The Society for the Advancement of Sexual Health.
   http://www.sash.net

Spring, J.A. (1996). *After the Affair: Healing the Pain and Rebuilding Trust When a Partner Has Been Unfaithful*. New York, NY: Perennial.

Staheli, L. (1995). *"Affair-Proof" Your Marriage: Understanding and Surviving an Affair*. New York, NY: Cliff Street Books.

Stradling, R. (1993). The Death of Don Juan: Murder, Myth, and Mayhem in Madrid. *History Today, 43*(5), 11-17.

Strauss, R.L. (1991). *Growing More Like Jesus: A Practical Guide to Developing a Christlike Character*. Neptune, NJ: Loizeaux.

Subotnik, R.B., & Harris, G.G. (2005). *Surviving Infidelity: Making Decisions, Recovering from the Pain*. (3rd ed.). Avon, MA: Adams Media.

Swenson, G. (1997). *Coping With Infidelity in Marriage*. Retrieved from: http://www.gregswensonphd.com/infidelity.htm#9

Thompson, M.J. (2002). *Companions In Christ: The Way of Forgiveness*. Nashville, TN: Upper Room Books.

Vaknin, S. (2008). *Malignant Self Love: Narcissism Revisited*. Prague, Czech Republic: Narcissus Publications.

Vaughan, P. (2003). *The Monogamy Myth: A Personal Handbook for Recovering from Affairs* (3rd ed.). New York, NY: New Market Press.

Vaughan, P. (2010). *Help for Therapists (and their Clients) in Dealing with Affairs*. San Diego, CA: Dialog Press.

Weatherhead, L.D. (1944). *The Will of God*. Nashville, TN: Abingdon Press.

Webster's Ninth New Collegiate Dictionary. (1983). Springfield, MA: Merriam-Webster Inc, Publishers.

Young, E. (2004). *Fatal Distractions*. Nashville, TN: Serendipity House.

About the Author

Dr. Deanna Sims received her doctoral and master's degrees in Counseling from the University of North Texas. She graduated Cum Laude from Texas A & M University with her undergraduate degree in Psychology.

Dr. Sims is a Licensed Professional Counselor in private practice in Dallas, Texas, and she provides individual, couples, family, and group therapy to adults with mental health or substance abuse issues.

In addition to Infidelity Recovery, Dr. Sims' other clinical interests include Mood Disorders, especially Bipolar Disorder, group therapy, grief and loss, infertility, and Cognitive Behavioral Therapy.

Dr. Sims presents lectures on Infidelity Recovery to mental health professionals and facilitates workshops and support groups for betrayed spouses and couples desiring to reconcile after an affair.

In her spare time, Dr. Sims enjoys baking, cake decorating, designing cards, gardening, studying the Bible, water skiing, and spending time with family and friends. She is an involved member of St. Andrew United Methodist Church and the Kings Ridge Ladies Bible Study, both in Plano, Texas. Dr. Sims participates in a Snack Ministry for the Homeless and Hungry. She lives in the Dallas area.

www.DrDeannaSims.com

Index to Scriptural References

K

I Kings 22:5 59
II Kings 22:13 5

L

Lamentations 3:25 113
Leviticus 19:18 39
Luke 24:46-47 12

M

Malachi 3:6 62
Mark 14:3–9 101
Matthew 5:4 63
Matthew 6:12 12
Matthew 6:27-28 23
Matthew 7:7-8 85
Matthew 16:19 88
Matthew 18:10-14 85
Matthew 18:20 105
Matthew 18:21-22 12
Matthew 22:37-38 7
Matthew 22:39 50, 89
Matthew 26:6–13 101
Matthew 27:46 88

N

Nehemiah 6:7 90
Numbers 14:18 6
Numbers 32:10-11 5
Numbers 32:13 5

P

I Peter 3:7 50
I Peter 4:10 61
Philippians 3:13-14 52
Philippians 4:6 48
Philippians 4:7 86
Philippians 4:13 13
Proverbs 5:15 3

Proverbs 11:12 50
Proverbs 11:14 90
Proverbs 11:17 50
Proverbs 12:5 90
Proverbs 12:19 51
Proverbs 14:30 43
Proverbs 20:11 110
Proverbs 29:11 6
Psalm 3:3 52
Psalm 10:14 63
Psalm 16:9 113
Psalm 17:6 84
Psalm 23:2-3 52
Psalm 30:5 6
Psalm 30:11 114
Psalm 32:3 57
Psalm 34:6 63
Psalm 39:7 113
Psalm 55:14 90
Psalm 56:8 47
Psalm 62:7 13
Psalm 71:14 113
Psalm 78:38 6
Psalm 78:39 13
Psalm 84:11 88
Psalm 111:1 105
Psalm 139:13-14 93

R

Revelation 5:8 47
Romans 5:3-5 112
Romans 8:28 52

S

I Samuel 2:2 62
Song of Songs 2:10 109
Song of Songs 2:16 108

T

I Timothy 2:1-2 48

Printed in the United States
By Bookmasters